This book is ^
the

CRIT

...HU SAYS SO?

Problem solving and communication skills

Don Pepperell

A
N
—
AU
—

Hutchinson Education

An imprint of Century Hutchinson Ltd
62–65 Chandos Place, London WC2N 4NW

Century Hutchinson Australia Pty Ltd
PO Box 496, 16–22 Church Street, Hawthorn, Melbourne,
Victoria 3122, Australia

Century Hutchinson New Zealand Limited
PO Box 40–086, Glenfield, Auckland 10,
New Zealand

Century Hutchinson South Africa (Pty) Ltd
PO Box 337, Bergvlei, 2012 South Africa

First published in 1988

Contents

Acknowledgements

This book is the result of nearly 10 years of teaching and it is therefore difficult to single out individuals and thank them for their contributions. I would, however, like to mention the following as having had some influence on its development and completion:

The staff and fellow students of Wolverhampton Technical Teachers' College who did their best to turn me into a teacher.

My colleagues at Corby Technical College and Moston College, Manchester.

John Beardshaw for his encouragement and editorial assistance.

All the students I have taught – good, bad and indifferent – who have prompted most of the ideas for this project.

Teresa for her patience and support.

For Mark and Keely

Preface

The aim of this book is to provide a context for a variety of communication skills. The subject matter has been chosen to build on students' basic knowledge in a range of areas while the exercises are intended to be progressively more complex. The activities are student-centred and provide back-up material for a wide range of courses including City and Guilds 362, B/TEC C&GS, YTS Life and Social Skills, CPVE and GCSE English. It has applications in both secondary schools and further education establishments.

It is *not* intended to be a course book. The emphasis is on student-centred activities involving skills in discussion, problem solving and communication; transferable skills which can apply to many subjects and courses. I make no apologies for using what might be regarded as a traditional general studies approach. I believe that useful, relevant and interesting topics which apply to a wider context than vocational training are perfectly valid, whatever the current fashion in course structures may be.

Specific objectives are included at the beginning of each chapter, while the general aim is to develop the student's awareness that

(a) there are many points of view to be brought to bear on a given issue;
(b) other people's opinions are based, for them, on valid concepts;
(c) seeking a variety of viewpoints is a desirable and worthwhile way of examining issues or solving problems.

In other words, many heads are better than one.

It should be added that this approach is in no way intended to create anarchy in the classroom, nor is it intended to encourage deeper entrenchment of individual attitudes and prejudices. Instead the idea is to develop a concensus with which all the students can at least partially agree.

Themes

1

Hidden meanings

By the end of this chapter the student should be able to:
1 Recognise that perception is based on prior, personal experience.
2 Recognise that a variety of language, oral and visual forms can be used to reinforce attitudes.
3 Assess the extent to which prior assumptions brought to a situation can limit possible courses of action.
4 Recognise that facts cannot be taken in isolation but need interpretation.
5 Define stereotypes.

Read the following very short story:

> When the police and ambulance arrived at the scene of the crash it was obvious that the driver of the car was dead, the teenage passenger was badly injured. The ambulance rushed the passenger to hospital. He had severe head injuries. The police soon discovered that the dead driver was the father of the injured boy.
>
> At the hospital the nurses treated his injuries as best they could but it was obvious that he needed an operation. The hospital's brain surgeon was called for while the patient was prepared for the operating theatre. Then the brain surgeon arrived, took one look at the boy lying on the bed and said:
>
> 'I can't operate on this boy. This is my son.'

If you found this story confusing, don't worry. You're not the only one. Yet the important facts are all there and it is quite straightforward. But if you *were* confused it is because you read the *facts* contained in the story then added some *meaning* of your own. This is something we all do, and the meaning would be based on your experiences. Most of the time doing this helps us to understand situations but it can sometimes cause problems.

▶ ▶ ▶ ▶ SOMETHING TO DO

Look at the photographs below and write down what you think is happening, including what you think has happened so far and what you think may happen next. *There is no right or wrong answer. Use humour if you like, but try to make the description fit the picture.*

When you have finished describe your own version of the story to the rest of the class or group. Did you all come up with the same story? If not, why not?

▶ ▶ ▶ ▶ THE POINT IS . . .

Even though we may see exactly the same thing we do not always put exactly the same **interpretation** on it.

If you watch sport on television there is always a commentator talking about the action while it is happening. The commentary provides information, such as the names of the players or an explanation of the rules, but there will also be an *interpretation* of the action for you: 'That was a *good* shot,' 'That was a *bad* tackle,' and so on. This is similar to what your mind does for you. It adds *meaning* to raw *facts*.

Of course, it can be very useful to us to be able to interpret what we see or hear going on. It is often essential. If you see a car coming towards you at great speed you do not wait to see if it will hit you before deciding what to do because (a) you assume that it will hit you if you don't move and (b) you assume that if it does hit you it will injure or kill you.

We react this way because we have *previously* learned the possible dangers of road traffic – cats, dogs and very young children are often victims of a lack of such knowledge.

● And if you are still confused by the story on page 7 it is because you assumed that the brain surgeon must be a man; she is in fact the boy's mother.

But how much do you think you know about *people*?

Are there any times when you *can* tell what people are like by their appearance? Suggest a few and discuss in groups or as a class what clues people can give to their jobs, their leisure interests, their likes and dislikes.

In particular, you might include such things as
● dress,
● accent,
● age,
● where they live,
● what kind of car they drive (if at all) and so on
● OR . . .

▶ ▶ ▶ ▶ **SOMETHING TO DO**

You could expand on this idea with a survey.

When interviewers do surveys for Gallup, Mori and Marplan they are often asked to choose people from a complete range of social backgrounds so as to make the findings as accurate as possible. This means that they have to try to guess what jobs they do, how old they are and what their income level might be *before* they have even spoken to them.

The people questioned are then placed in what is known as a 'socio-economic group', which is an attempt, basically, to put a definite measure on what is normally called 'social class'.

Here is a general list of these socio-economic groups:

A. Higher Professional and Executive: judges, university lecturers, top civil servants, surgeons, company directors and the like.
B. Professional and Managerial: teachers, managers and business men and women, social workers, etc.
C1. Intermediate Non-manual: technicians, supervisors, clerical workers.
C2. Skilled Manual: bricklayers, electricians, carpenters, welders, motor mechanics, toolmakers, etc.
D. Other Manual Workers: semi- and unskilled.
E. Other: unemployed, old age pensioners (on a state pension), students, etc.

The idea of these groups is to sort out not only how much they earn but also to take into account social background, spending habits and general social outlook. For example, while a self-employed builder may earn more than a vicar he is less likely to read the *Times*, go to the theatre or drink wine.

The questioner also takes into account the family. If a woman describes herself as a housewife then the interviewer will ask her what her husband does for a living – in other words, her social grouping is taken as that of the chief wage-earner.

Thus you could now try a double exercise:

1. Conduct a survey, such as the smoking one in Chapter 7, or one of your own. Try to make it *representative* by asking people in set proportions from the socio-economic groups. To simplify it, you could place them in categories A + B, C1 + C2, and D + E. A reasonable ratio would be: A/B – 25%: C1/C2 – 40%: D/E – 35%.

2. To do this you will need to estimate which group the people questioned come from *before* you ask the questions. You will have to look for clues, such as dress and general appearance, which you think will help you to place that person in a particular social category. When you ask the questions, you can find out, from their job, which group they actually belong to. Then, if one group from the class goes out with the intention of asking only A/Bs and comes back with, say, four from the C1/C2 group and sixteen A/Bs, their success rate would be 80 per cent.

You might like to use a form with your questionnaire similar to this:

TARGET GROUP (A/B, C1/C2, D/E)

OCCUPATION .... = ACTUAL GROUP ....

SEX M ☐ F ☐

AGE 16–25 ☐ 26–35 ☐ 36–45 ☐ 46–55 ☐ 56–65 ☐ RETIRED

Then add any other information you might like to know such as whether the person is a home-owner or car owner or any other indicator of their social status. Then do the survey.

What you are looking for is information which can give an overall picture of the people answering the questions. Then *correlations* can be made – whether professional people are more or less likely to smoke, whether manual workers are more likely to vote Labour, and so on.

And one final point about the way people look:

DID YOU KNOW?
When he entered a contest to find his lookalike, Charlie Chaplin came third.
(*Daily Mirror*, 17 Jan. 1987)

As we grow up we gradually get used to the sights and sounds of the world around us. Eventually most of it becomes familiar – so familiar that we tend to see shape and depth in simple collections of straight lines, as in the pictures below.

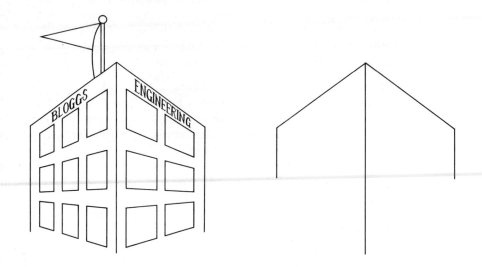

BUT because of this, we can also be fooled into seeing things which aren't there or being confused by what we see, as in the following examples.

Is there really a whiter, upside-down triangle in the middle of the other shapes?

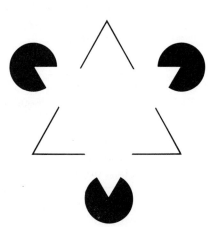

Are there two black lines here?
Are they straight?

Are the two black lines in a straight line?

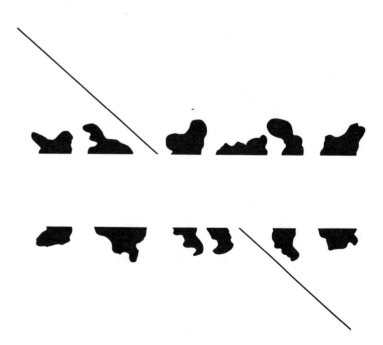

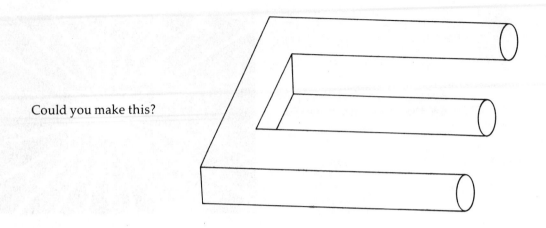

Could you make this?

And why does the black line on
the right appear to be longer than
the one on the left?

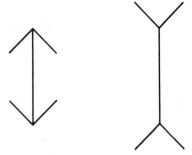

▶ ▶ ▶ ▶ **SOMETHING TO DO**

Now that your mind is 'loosened up' perhaps you can attempt to solve the following problems. There are not any *right* answers necessarily, but some are neater or better than others.

1 Connect up the dots in the least number of straight lines. Once you start drawing the lines you cannot take the pen off the paper. (That is, the line must be continuous.) The lines must pass through all of the dots and if you go back over the same line, that counts as two.

   What's the least you can do it in?

2 Move two counters so that you end up with five counters in a straight line across the page and five counters in a straight line down the page at the same time.

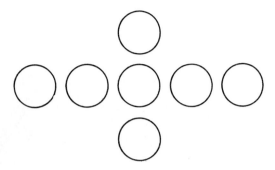

3 A farmer is on his way home with a bag of corn, a chicken and a dog. The only reason the dog does not eat the chicken and that the chicken does not eat the corn is that the farmer is there to stop them. But he has to cross a river in a very small, old boat. This boat can only take the weight of the farmer plus one other item or it will sink so he will have to leave two of them together at a time while he is crossing the river. How can he get them all across without the dog eating the chicken or the chicken eating the corn?

4 Arrange six matches to form four equilateral triangles.

5 The diagram shows a ping-pong ball in a tube. The tube is embedded in a concrete floor. In the room with you are:

- A box of cornflakes
- A wire coat hanger
- A file
- A chisel
- A hammer
- A pair of pliers
- A book
- 100 ft of rope

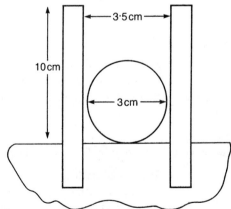

Your task is to get the ping-pong ball out of the tube without damaging the tube, the ball or the floor. How would you do it?

Remember: ANY solution is acceptable. Some may just be quicker or easier than others. Don't forget humour.

Consider all the problems on your own for a while then discuss them as a class. You may find that other people have come up with things you hadn't thought of. Then again, your answer might be the 'best'. Some suggested answers are given at the end of this chapter (p. 23).

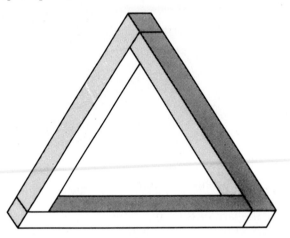

▶ ▶ ▶ ▶ THE POINT IS . . .

Things are not always as they seem. We can sometimes find ourselves trapped in a very narrow way of thinking because we make many assumptions. It often takes a real effort to accept that things do not always fall neatly into our own version of what the world is like. Prejudice, for example, can cloud our judgment. Some men are unhappy at having a woman for their boss. Some people dislike foreigners simply because they are foreigners.

▶ ▶ ▶ ▶ FACT

In the 1936 Olympic games in Germany Jesse Owens, a black American, won four gold medals. This greatly upset Adolf Hitler who for years had preached that white races were superior to blacks, Jews and orientals. He stormed out of the stadium in disgust.

▶ ▶ ▶ ▶ THINKING IS A SKILL

Just like reading, talking, riding a bicycle or building a brick wall, thinking is something that you can train yourself to do.

Edward de Bono is the man who coined the term 'Lateral Thinking'. He believes in the possibility of teaching people to think. One of the exercises he uses is to present a situation and then ask people to consider the different viewpoints of those involved, such as the story of an eagle that has escaped from a zoo. The viewpoints may be as follows:

The zoo-keeper – I must get the bird back as quickly as possible. This could give the zoo a bad reputation. This is ridiculous, climbing up trees after birds. Someone is to blame for leaving the cage open.

A journalist – I hope they don't catch the bird just yet; this story could go on for a long time. Can I get close enough for a good picture? Who else can I involve from the public; maybe they'll give me some ideas on how to catch the bird.

The public – Funny to see all these people having so much trouble catching a bird. Hope the bird escapes for good – animals should be free, not locked up in cages. Can I show how clever I am by catching the bird for them?

The eagle – What's all this fuss about? Funny not having bars all around me. I'm hungry. Where shall I go next?

Much of what follows in this book is based on this idea, so here's . . .

▶ ▶ ▶ ▶ SOMETHING TO DO

Imagine that there is a proposal to open a new youth club on a housing estate. In groups of three or four discuss and then write down what you think the viewpoints of the following people might be:

- The young people on the estate.
- The police.
- A local community worker.
- The local shopkeepers.
- The parents of the youngsters on the estate.

When you have come up with a number of different viewpoints, explain them to the rest of the class. Are there any your group did not think of?

You may also find that what is thought to be an advantage of the scheme by one person is a disadvantage to someone else.

This is a technique that can be developed to cover all situations where a conflict may arise. If you practise it enough it will become possible for you to do this on your own and still come up with a variety of points of view.

BUT . . .

It is one thing to be able to see the other point of view – it is quite another to bring yourself to agree with it.

This is what *prejudice* is all about. Prejudice is an attitude of mind that makes us act in a set way in a given situation.

For example:

- If you are a racist you will tend to look for those things you see as bad in people of a different nationality or colour. You will ignore their good qualities. This way of seeing people will then strengthen your prejudice.
- If you support a particular sports team it is unlikely that you will completely agree with a journalist who writes a report criticizing them, even if you weren't at the game.
- How often have you heard people argue about the type of music they like? Is the argument likely to change anyone's mind?

Prejudice goes hand in hand with *stereotypes*.

A stereotype is a *general* image we have of certain people or things that makes it difficult to see the *individual*.

Here are some examples:

- Women are bad drivers.
- Young people today aren't as disciplined as people were fifty years ago.
- The Irish are thick.
- Americans are brash.
- Germans are arrogant.

So what image or stereotype do you have of the following? Write down two or three words to describe each of them:

- Politicians
- Bosses
- The police
- Teachers
- Nurses
- Football supporters
- Trade unions
- Australians
- Ballet dancers
- People who write books like this one

Now discuss your reasons for the descriptions you chose.

You may find that there were disagreements over your descriptions. This is normal because we all approach situations from our own viewpoint. There is nothing wrong with having a point of view. It only becomes a problem when you believe that *your* point of view must always be *right* for everyone else.

The rest of this book is designed to illustrate some of the situations in which different viewpoints may cause confusion or conflict. The intention is not to try to make you change your opinions or your personality – after all, as the author I have to accept that I may be wrong – but to make you understand that seeing as many points of view as possible can help us all to make fewer snap judgements and more good decisions.

▶ ▶ ▶ ▶ **SOMETHING TO DO**

Each member of the class should write on a piece of paper about six things they think describe them – *not* their appearance, but their personality. There is a list of words below to help you. Then hand the paper to your teacher who will read them out. Do you think the rest of the class will be able to recognise you from your description of yourself?

Personality characteristics:
intelligent friendly quick-tempered shy likeable ambitious humorous easy-going argumentative serious happy-go-lucky forgetful lazy helpful kind hard-working cheerful quiet talkative popular

and so on. These are only suggestions and you can add to them by using words such as 'very' or 'quite' (e.g. 'quite serious' or 'very talkative') to make the description more accurate.

▶ ▶ ▶ ▶ **THE POINT IS . . .**

It doesn't matter too much if you have faults provided you are aware of them. There's nothing worse than thinking you are the nicest person in the world if nobody else thinks so. You may have problems in life if you do not know what other people think of you.

If you want something light to read that comically illustrates this point about prejudices and the mistakes people can make from making assumptions about each other, try 'Krumnagel' by Peter Ustinov. It is the story of an American cop on holiday in England who shoots a man in a pub during an argument. The story of the trial is very funny.

The numbers game

No, this isn't a section on maths. But it is about numbers and the way people use them.

Benjamin Disraeli, Prime Minister over 100 years ago, is supposed to have said that there are three kinds of untruth – Lies, Damn Lies and Statistics.

Not that there is anything wrong with statistics if we know how they are put together. It's just that when people come to *interpret* those numbers they may read more into them than is actually there.

Look at the following examples. For each one try to work out what is wrong with them and why you think that particular meaning is being put on them or why they are misleading. See p. 23 for the 'answers'.

1 'In tests, eight out of ten owners who expressed a preference said their cats preferred it.' (It may help you to know that when the advert first came out it simply said, 'In tests, eight out of ten owners said their cats preferred it.')
2 Try this one – preferably with a friend and not with the serious intention of winning money. You each have a coin which you toss. If both coins come down 'heads' your opponent wins. If they both come down tails, you win. If they come down one head and one tail, you also win. However, because you have two chances in three to win, and your opponent only has one in three, you will pay him or her twice the amount of the bet. In other words, if you are playing for 10p stakes you receive 10p, but if your opponent wins you pay 20p. On pure chance you should both come out even – shouldn't you?
3 'On average it rains on seven days out of the thirty in June. Since we've already had eight days of rain this June so far and it's only the 20th, I'll be okay to leave my raincoat at home for the rest of the month.'
4 A public opinion poll conducted in New York some years ago predicted a large win for the Republican candidate at a presidential election. The survey was done

by picking people purely at random from the telephone book and ringing them up to ask them how they intended to vote. The Democrat candidate won. What went wrong with the survey?

5 Most road accidents happen within 3 miles of the driver's home. You are probably, therefore, much safer travelling long distances than you are driving to work.

6 And similarly, one accident in five involves a driver who has been drinking. That means that *four* out of five involve sober drivers. It is therefore safer to drive if you have had a few drinks.

7 A psychologist once did a survey and found that there was a direct relationship between the size of children's feet and their scores in an intelligence test.

8 The following diagrams and charts are the sort you might find people using to back up a point they want to make. Can you find what's wrong with them?

(a) In their annual accounts Clearview Double Glazing Ltd claim, 'It can be seen from the figures that we are continuing to increase our profits steadily.' Are they?

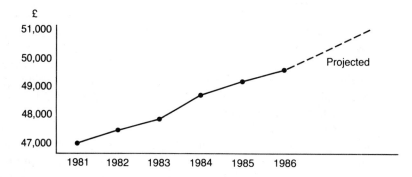

(b) Two political parties are given the same figures for economic growth over the last 10 years. They come up with the following graphs for their party political broadcasts. Who is telling the truth?

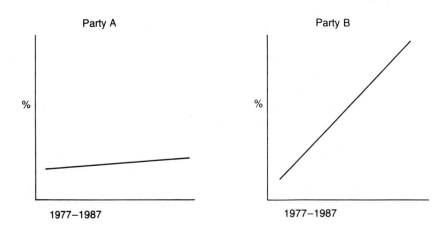

One of the problems with numbers is that they seem to be definite: $2 + 2 = 4$ and that's it. It's not an opinion, it's a fact. But the problem arises when people try to prove or disprove something which *is* an opinion by using factual information such as mathematics.

For example, over 450 years ago a man called Nicolas Copernicus took a series of measurements of the movement of the planets and found that the results did not fit in with the accepted idea that they revolved around the earth. A work published after his death suggested that the earth in fact went round the sun. Years later Galileo Galilei proved this mathematically and was imprisoned for daring to suggest such a thing. In this case, instead of juggling the figures to prove a point, he interpreted them correctly but was not liked for it because the results went against accepted ideas at the time.

Perhaps this kind of thing is what puts people off ideas that are backed up by facts and figures. If they don't like the truth then people will claim that the figures have been 'rigged'. And, of course, when it perhaps turns out that the figures *have* been rigged, it makes people even more suspicious.

So what is the point of all this?

Well, it is a sad fact that people will use statistics to give their arguments an air of truth and respectability – after all, you can't argue with facts, can you?

But statistics are often misused because they are misunderstood. For example, certain political groups use the 'facts' that in Britain there are about 3 million unemployed people and also about 3 million black people to 'prove' that black immigrants are taking our jobs and that if we sent them 'home' (wherever that may be) we could solve the unemployment problem.

This completely ignores the other facts which are:

- Many of the unemployed are black. In fact in percentage terms, unemployment is worse among black people, so how can they be taking our jobs?
- If all the black people left Britain we would also lose the money they spend. This would depress industry even further and *cause* unemployment.
- There were 3 million people unemployed in Britain in the 1930s when there were very few black people here at all.

But if you are a racist it is very tempting to use such simple information to prove your point of view.

▶ ▶ ▶ ▶ **SOMETHING TO DO**

Look at the following facts and figures, then answer the questions on them.

Wizard Prang Insurance Services Ltd: Annual Statistical Review.
A: Car accidents by speed of vehicle at time of accident and cost of repair.

Cost of repair	Speed of insured's vehicle in mph					
	Under 15	16–30	31–40	41–55	56–70	Total
under £200	27	14	5	2	1	49
£201–£500	21	27	18	10	3	79
£501–£1,000	15	35	26	9	16	101
£1,501–£2,000	8	33	16	27	28	112
£2,001–£3,000	11	21	11	37	36	116
Over £3,000	3	17	14	14	21	69
Write-offs	34	19	12	22	17	104
Total	128	209	131	125	135	728

Total cost of repairs = £1,117,682
Total number of insured persons = 6,365
Total receipts from premiums = £1,233,218.70
Gross profit on car insurance = £115,536.70

1 What percentage of insured drivers made a claim in this year? (Assume that the company accepted all claims and paid for repairs.)
2 What was the average cost of repairs?
3 What was the average premium paid by drivers?

This is of course a very simple example and does not include such things as 'excesses' – that is, payments made by drivers for the first £25, £50, etc. of the cost of repairs. You can 'play around with' the figures and come up with all sorts of possibly useful answers, such as the profit margin on car insurance, but do the figures reveal anything else about driving and drivers in general?
Can you, for example, answer the following questions?

1 Do low-speed or high-speed accidents cost the most to put right?
2 Can you work out (roughly) what the average cost of a 'write-off' is?
3 What does this depend on?
4 Is there any consistent pattern in the way speed relates to cost? Would you expect there to be one?

Make a note of the answers to the above questions and also note down what information you think may be missing from the table, or even incorrect. Remember that this information would be taken from claim forms filled in by drivers.

Answers to questions

Pages 14–15
1 It can be done in four lines
   (Did you stay inside the imaginary square?)

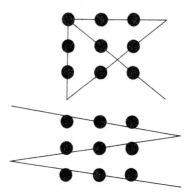

or three, like this.
(Did you only think of going through the
centre of the dots?)

2 Move the two outside coins of the row of five and place them *on top* of the coin in the centre. The key to this is thinking in *three* dimensions.
3 Step 1: Take the chicken across.
   Step 2: Return, then take the dog across.
   Step 3: Return *with the chicken* and leave it there.
   Step 4: Take the corn across and leave it with the dog.
   Step 5: Go back and get the chicken.
      If you had any difficulty with this it is probably because you did not consider bringing anything back with you.
4 Like 2, think in three dimensions as shown:

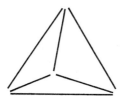

5 This is just a test of your creativity and imagination, but did you forget that *you* were in the room? If you did think of urinating into the tube then, while it might not seem to be very pleasant, at least you can take an extra mark for not being bound by social conventions.

Pages 19–20

1 The 'expressed a preference' gives it away. If 80 per cent of owners really did think that Whiskas was the best then that company would sell nearly all the cat food on the market. But they don't. It is, however, perfectly possible that when they did the survey the results came out something like this:

  They asked 100 people and 16 said their cat preferred Whiskas, 2 said they preferred Kit-E-Kat, and 2 others named some other brand. The other 80 may have said that their cat would eat anything at all. So 16 out of 100 could become 8 out of 10 for the advertiser's purposes.

2 Your opponent's chances of winning are, simply, not one in three but one in *four*. There are four combinations – 2 heads, 2 tails, 1 head and a tail, *and 1 tail and a head*.

3 You cannot use statistics of what has happened in the past to predict what will happen in the future – especially with the English weather. The *average* is probably the most abused statistic known.

4 The problem with the phone survey was that it was biased from the start. People who had telephones at that time were likely to be well off; and the Republican Party has more support among wealthy people. This meant that large numbers of Democrat supporters were not even asked since they did not have telephones.

5 Most accidents happen within 3 miles of home because most journeys take place within that distance.

6 Or, looked at another way, if there were no drunks on the road then 100 per cent of accidents would involve sober drivers. What this does not tell us is whether there would be *fewer accidents in total* if there were no drunk drivers about.

7 This is a common mistake – suggesting that one thing *causes* another. In fact bigger feet and better test scores are both caused by the same thing – age. The children with the bigger feet were older.

8 (a) Clearview Double Glazing may be increasing their profits but not by anywhere near as much as the slope of the graph would suggest. If you were to draw the graph with the missing £46,000 below the line, the slope would look negligible. Profits are increasing by about 1% per year, which is below the rate of inflation and the company is therefore doing *worse* each year.

  (b) Because there are no scales shown at all, the graphs are meaningless. They could both just as easily apply to a 1% growth rate as a 50% growth rate.

2

Well, what do you know?

By the end of this chapter the student should be able to:

1 Assess the aims of education.

2 Suggest a definition of educational success or failure.

3 Examine the influences on the planning and implementation of the curriculum.

4 Evaluate the role of education in socialization.

5 Assess his/her own attitudes to education and suggest reasons for them.

We can get our information and opinions from a number of sources – family, friends, the mass media and, of course, school. They all have different effects on us and we learn different types of things from each of them.

Of course, they are not completely separate. For example, you might think that it is your parents' job to teach you manners, but of course the school will also carry this teaching on.

So what exactly is the education system there for?

Ours is a complicated society and as we grow up we need many different skills to be able to cope. Try to imagine, for example, how difficult or different our daily lives would be if we could not read or write, or do basic calculations.

This is the basis of what school teaches us – reading, writing and arithmetic, or the '3 Rs' as they are sometimes known.

While we might accept that English and Maths are the normal, basic subjects we all have to take at school, it is a fact that the only subjects schools *must* teach are Religious Education and Physical Education. But since we do not want a society which consists entirely of priests who are good at athletics, we offer a wider range of things to study. Because school is there to prepare us for our adult lives, and since our role in life may depend a great deal on what we do for a living, the subjects we study are aimed at making us *useful* members of society.

But how do we decide on what is useful?

▶ ▶ ▶ ▶ **SOMETHING TO DO**

Below is a chart showing a number of school subjects. First place them in order of importance by putting a number next to them in the first column – that is, if you think English is the most important put a 1 next to it, and so on through all the subjects. (It may be easier for discussion afterwards if you do this in small groups.) Try to avoid putting the subjects you *like* high on the list just because you like them. Then, in the next column, write in why you think the subject is studied at all.

Subject	Importance	Reason for studying it
English		
Maths		
History		
Physics		
Geography		
Chemistry		

(continued)

Subject	Importance	Reason for studying it
French (or other foreign language)		
Biology		
Social Studies		
Home economics		
Craft, Design and Technology		
Computer studies		
Sex Education		

Now discuss as a class how you chose the order of importance.

In other words, you are discussing what makes a subject worth studying?

Did you find it difficult to come up with 'reasons for studying' a particular subject?

If so, why?

► ► ► ► **THE POINT IS . . .**

There are many reasons given about how and why certain things are done in education, but they often come down to two main ones:

1 Education is about preparing people for work and making them valuable to a society in *economic* terms.
2 Education is about preparing people for adult life and should include making them valuable to society as a whole in moral, social and economic terms.

In practice there is always an element of both in the decisions about what is taught in school.

Further education is slightly different. Technical colleges have grown up out of the needs of industry and the training of apprentices, although their work has changed and grown in recent years. But the emphasis has mostly been on *training* for a definite job.

So how do people decide on what to include in a course of study?

► ► ► ► **SOMETHING TO DO**

Put yourself in the position of people who are affected by such a decision and decide on the subjects you would include in a course or set of courses.

You will need to divide into four groups and each group will look at the problem from a particular viewpoint. The groups are:

1 The local chamber of commerce (i.e. local employers)
2 Teachers
3 The students/school pupils
4 The parents of the students

● In your group decide on what *you* as these people would want to see on the timetable *in school*. Remember that you are limited for time by the normal school timetable so use one that you are familiar with.

 Some subjects may seem obvious but with others you will need to be ready to justify your choice to the rest of the class.

 Would you include any groups of subjects which are optional, that is, at a particular time of the week students can choose between a number of subjects?

 Would you 'stream' students for different exams?

 Would you separate the subjects into humanities, science and social science?

● When you have decided on your basic timetable (remember to show how many lessons per week would be spent on each subject) present it to the rest of the class and then discuss your proposals.

 Did you reach agreement?

 Chances are that you all included certain 'core' subjects such as English and Maths, but disagreed on others.

 Did you, for example, find that students went for a different type of content from that wanted by local employers?

 Did you find yourselves staying with the type of subjects that you have studied up to now?

Did you find yourselves putting in options that were different for boys and girls?

Perhaps you can do a similar exercise for the course that you are on now. Would it be very different?

The reason for asking you to look at the school curriculum was that it forms the basis of anything else you do from then on.

Of course anything you may have decided on will still involve the argument about whether subjects are

- Interesting
- Worth studying for their own sake
- Relevant
- Useful

When looking at the reasons behind the way subjects are chosen in schools and colleges, we are assuming that at the end of it all there is some way of measuring how good we are at those subjects.

Most people feel that we ought to *assess* a person's ability through some kind of testing or examination. Our success or otherwise in this will then be used by other people, such as employers, to decide how much ability (or lack of it) we may have.

Does that sound reasonable?

One of the problems with testing people is that we may find that we are testing something other than a particular subject. You may have a brilliant grasp of history, for example, but if you cannot write down what you know you will not pass the exam. It is therefore not just your knowledge and understanding that is being tested but your ability to *communicate* that knowledge to others.

Would you be surprised to hear that a person's home background may be at least as important as any ability he or she might have when it comes to doing well at school?

Surprised or not, there is a lot of evidence to suggest that this is true. It is a fact that the son of a bank manager is much more likely to go on to higher education (and usually a better paid job) than the daughter of a factory labourer. Forgetting about individuals for the moment it is true that *in general* the higher a family's social status, the better the children do at school.

► ► ► ► TALKING POINT

- Does this mean that better-off people give birth to naturally more intelligent children?
- Could it be that the schools and other educational institutions are simply testing our ability to be 'middle class'?

► ► ► ► SOMETHING TO DO

Overleaf are some facts about educational achievement.

In small groups or individually, try to work out some of the reasons for the differences.

Ability will obviously count, but for how much?

In what ways can it be an advantage to be born into a small, white, middle-class family?

Remember that we are talking about people who are comfortably off and who send their children to *state* schools. Very wealthy people may choose to send their children to a private school but this only amounts to about 5 per cent of all school children. There are still large differences *within* the state system.

Percentage of children from state schools entering higher education by IQ at age 11 and father's occupation:

IQ	Father's occupation	Enter full-time higher education (%)
130 and over	Non-manual	41
	Manual	30
115–129	Non-manual	34
	Manual	15
100–114	Non-manual	17
	Manual	6

Some facts about children from fee-paying (private) schools:

About 5 per cent of children actually go to 'public school' yet they

- make up over 70 per cent of judges
  over 60 per cent of top Foreign Office officials
  over 80 per cent of army generals and navy admirals and
- have nineteen times as great a chance of going to Oxford or Cambridge Universities than children from state schools.

▶ ▶ ▶ ▶ TALKING POINTS

There have been a number of theories put forward to explain these differences. Perhaps the answers to the following questions will help you to decide.

The home
- Do middle-class parents encourage their children more because they themselves believe in the value of a good education?
- Do they have more money to spend on books and educational trips to museums and the like?
- Do middle-class parents start their children's education earlier by being able to devote more time and attention to them *before* they go to school?
- People who are better off have more choice about where to live because they can afford to buy their house. Does this mean that the children will be brought up in a more pleasant environment; and can the parents choose to live near a school with higher standards?

● Can the size of the family affect a child's chances?

The school
● Is the school building likely to be in better condition in middle-class suburbs than in the inner cities?
● Does the wealth of an area rub off on the school, allowing better resources in the 'middle-class' schools?
● Do teachers treat working-class children differently, expecting less from them and therefore giving them less attention?
● Can the way you speak (with a strong local accent or using slang expressions) give the teachers the impression that you are not very clever?
● Does streaming in schools mean that the working-class children (who start off with poorer communication skills and therefore end up in the lower groups) give up at an early age?
● Are the subjects themselves 'loaded' in favour of middle-class children because they are more suited to jobs like teaching and office work than they are to manual jobs like bricklaying? And are middle-class children brought up to expect that they will go into non-manual jobs and therefore see more point in doing well at school?

A lot of questions with no easy answers. But in general they are thought to be the kinds of things that affect the way children see school. After all, if you go to school with the idea that education is something that other people are good at, the chances are that you will not achieve as much as you can.

And there are two things which have not been mentioned up to now – race and sex.

Do you think that being black or being a girl can be a disadvantage at school?

Whatever your views on why some people do better at school than others, you cannot escape the fact that at some time you are going to leave. When you do there are people who will want to know how you got on. And in general it is paper qualifications that are most used to show what you have managed to achieve.

They can be used in two main ways:

1 They show a level of ability in a definite area, such as maths or science, which is *directly relevant* to a particular job.
2 They show a general ability to learn. History or Latin may not be of use in most jobs but your knowledge of them proves that you *can* be taught to a certain level.

So what is intelligence?

One way of measuring this is by IQ tests (IQ stands for Intelligence Quotient) but many people believe that these tests only measure your ability to do IQ tests. Here are a couple of examples:

● Which is the odd person out?
RZATOM PHINCO HEVETNOBE GRELA YBLAGE

● Which is the odd one out?
CMTEO GUANDRAV BENAMUS LHIMNAL MOCERM

Obviously they are anagrams you need to solve before you can decide which one is the odd one out. But when you do work them out, you may still not know the answer because you do not know anything about classical music or 30-year-old cars and jet aircraft.

Does this mean that you are less intelligent than someone who does?

As we have already seen, it may not be just knowledge and your ability to use it which is important; it is the *type* of knowledge which is thought by some to be an important guide to your abilities.

But is it right to assume that what we learn at school is being used to steer us into a particular job when we eventually leave?

You may have noticed that most of this book is about topics or subjects not directly necessary for work. If you are on a course of training for a job most of what you study is to help you to do that job properly.

But education in its widest sense is about life in general. One of the earlier exercises in this chapter was about the subjects you study at school and whether they are useful or 'relevant'. Let's look at this from a different point of view.

▶ ▶ ▶ ▶ SOMETHING TO DO

Imagine that exams have been abolished and replaced by a system in which teachers are given the job of simply writing a detailed report on you when you leave. Instead of dividing your achievements into subjects they have to give a general report on you as a person, including an opinion on whether you would make a good worker and in what sort of area (e.g. manual, clerical, working alone or dealing with people, etc.). It would then be the job of employers to give you the training in job skills later. (Ignore for now the difficulties that would arise if a teacher was biased against certain individuals.)

Divide into small groups and

1 Draw up a list of the things which you think should be included in the report.
   What *specific abilities* would you include?
   In other words, would you still give an assessment under headings like Maths and English as well as, say, behaviour and attitudes?
2 When you have done this, discuss your list as a class. This should then give you a wide enough range to work on the next task.
3 Draw up a list of subjects you would like to see included on the school timetable.
   Instead of thinking just in terms of useful and relevant to work, list the subjects under the following headings:
   ● Basic skills which will be useful for all types of work and adult life.
   ● Social skills.
   ● Topics of general usefulness, which include bringing in a range of 'subjects'. For example, 'The Environment' could include science, politics, crafts and communications.
   ● Activities or topics of use to you as a person. These could range from sports to community involvements.

Show how many hours you would give to each and be prepared to justify your choices to the rest of the class.

▶ ▶ ▶ ▶ **TALKING POINT**

Now discuss your new curriculum as a class using the following questions as a guide.

- Did you find that trying to get away from traditional school subjects (if you did, that is) produced a different look to the timetable?
- Do you think that children would enjoy school more under your system?
- Do you think such a system would be fairer to children who were not 'academic'?
- Would it be likely to raise or lower educational standards?
- What do you think employers would think of such a system?
- Would it be better for society as a whole (i.e. would we all leave school as 'nicer' people)?

3

Who do you think you are?

By the end of this chapter the student should be able to:

1 Recognise the extent to which role is dependent on social context.
2 Suggest the ways in which we learn social roles.
3 Examine the reasons for the post-war growth in recognisable youth cultures.
4 Assess the extent to which changes in role bring about changes in behaviour.
5 Assess the importance of stereotypes in our perceptions of other people.

Every one of us is an individual, which means that in some way or other we are different from everyone else, and some of those differences are great. But we are also quite like other people in many ways and this fact is what keeps society as a whole together. For example:

- Some people would argue that football hooliganism is a problem in modern Britain. Yet every week over a half a million people go along and pay money to watch a game. Nearly 3 million play.
- Nearly every home in Britain has a television set. Most of us spend many hours watching it, even though we often complain about what is on.
- Less than half the people in the country agree with the government of the time, whichever party is in power, yet nearly everyone supports the system of democracy which put them there.
- And so on . . .

In other words while we may be different in some ways, most of us *conform* to what the rest of society wants. In Chapter 5 we shall be looking at what happens when people break loose from the controls on them but for now it is worth asking what happens to us to make us behave the way we do.

Try the following questions – and try to be honest in your answers.

Answer the questions with a yes/no/maybe but then on the right fill in, as far as you know, *why* you think you feel this way.

	Yes/no/ maybe	WHY?
1. Are you patriotic?	....	....
2. Are you frightened of the dark?	....	....
3. Do you, or did you, like school?	....	....
4. Do you like classical music?	....	....
5. Do you like politics?	....	....
6. Do you want to get married?	....	....
7. Would you like to be rich?	....	....
8. Do you like animals?	....	....
9. Do you dislike foreigners?	....	....
10. Do you always obey the law?	....	....
11. Do you smoke?	....	....
12. Are you usually polite?	....	....
13. Do you read books regularly?	....	....
14. Do you give to charity?	....	....
15. Do you respect your elders?	....	....

Now discuss your answers with the rest of the class. Were any questions answered the same way by everyone? Were there any unusual answers?

▶ ▶ ▶ ▶ **THE POINT IS . . .**

It really doesn't matter too much whether you answered yes or no to the questions, but you may have found it difficult to say *why* you feel the way you do. You may just think of it as 'natural'.

You may also have noticed that other people in the class do not have the views you take for granted – people who say they are not patriotic, for example, when you are sure this is the only way to be.

But there really is nothing 'natural' about many of the attitudes we take for granted. We have to learn them.

Can you think of anything which you know or believe which did not come from

- Your family (or the people who brought you up)
- Your friends
- School
- The media (television, newspapers, magazines, adverts, etc.)

From the moment we are born we start to learn attitudes, and in a complex society like ours there are many influences on us that help to form them.

Since we know nothing when we are born we take things as they come afterwards, so that living in a house with Mum and Dad and perhaps a brother or sister seems 'natural'. Dad disappearing each day then coming back later while Mum stays with you and works around the house is quite normal. From the pattern of your family life and the things you see on television you start to build up a picture of the world. And as you grow older you come to realize that one day you will be independent and will need to build your own adult life. This will probably include marriage and a family of your own, perhaps your own house and a car and all the other things you think of as being normal and desirable.

And even if you don't want any of these things, something has happened at some time to make you feel this way.

Of course, this doesn't mean that we are all robots who have been programmed to live our lives in a set way. We do have choices and can make decisions, but these will be limited by the world we live in and the way we have learned to expect particular things from life.

The stereotypes mentioned in Chapter 1 are an example of how we try to make some sense out of what is going on around us. We don't have time to get to know everyone and so we may make judgements based on our own experiences and what we have been told by others.

Unfortunately not everyone will always agree with us, mainly because their experiences are different from ours.

> 'Who'll be my role model,
> Now that my role model has gone?'
> (From 'You Can Call Me Al' by Paul Simon)

When we do something as part of a general way of doing things which fits in with what other people expect of us, this could be said to be a *role*.

For example, 'a student' may be seen as casually, even scruffily, dressed; young; noisy; politically informed and active; intelligent but not necessarily well behaved; idealistic and out of touch with the 'real world'.

Whether this is accurate or not, some students may find this image attractive and live up (or down) to it. Hard working, smartly dressed and quiet youngsters may not be seen as students by many people.

So our role in life may come down to:

● doing what other people expect us to do;
● looking the way they expect us to look.

We're back to stereotypes again, but this time we may choose to live up to the image others expect to see.

▶ ▶ ▶ ▶ **SOMETHING TO DO**

Fill in your ideas on what people would do to fill the following roles. Look at it from *your* point of view – if you had to, how would you fill this role?

	Appearance	Behaviour
Teacher	....	....
Mum	....	....
Dad	....	....
Rock band singer	....	....
Judge	....	....
Burglar	....	....
Nurse	....	....
Son	....	....
Daughter	....	....
Scientist	....	....
Man	....	....
Woman	....	....
Police officer	....	....

▶ ▶ ▶ ▶ TALKING POINT

- Why did you feel this way? If you discuss your answers in the class you may find many similar answers and some differences.
- Did you get your impression of these roles from

  - What you know from experience?
  - What other people have told you personally?
  - Impressions gained from, say, television and newspapers?
  - Observation?

Of course, we all fit into different roles at different times. This often involves changing our behaviour to suit the circumstances. Let's take one example:

Joe Bloggs is a 41-year-old married man with two teenage children – a son who is 13 and a daughter who is 16. He is a service engineer with a computer sales company. His leisure time outside the home is usually taken up with golf and watching football.

Not a very detailed profile, but even this shows him in a number of different roles:

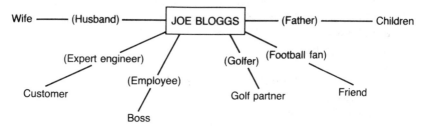

And each of them means that he will be a 'different person' while he is in that role:

- He would be unlikely to use the same kind of language with a customer as he might be tempted to use on the terraces at a football match.
- What he talks about on the golf course may be very different from conversations with the boss at work.
- He may not get on too well at work if he spoke to the boss the way he may sometimes speak to his children (even if he does feel that the boss is in the wrong).
- And so on . . .

You may have noticed that the relationships will vary with:

- How *formal* the situation is.
- Whether any *authority relationship* is involved.

And each role carries with it a *two-way* understanding of
- what he expects from other people;
- what they expect of him.

▶ ▶ ▶ ▶ SOMETHING TO DO

Draw a similar chart for yourself.

Make it clear, either by using different colours or a boxed type of layout, which are the formal and informal relationships and which ones involve some kind of authority.

Discuss your chart in class.

Are there any major differences?

Why?

Rock and role

One of the areas where Joe Bloggs might run into difficulties is in the role of parent. In the last 40 years or so one of the more obvious social changes has been among teenagers; and their impact on society has grown.

Not that teenagers are a recent invention, but other changes (such as the raising of the school leaving age or the growing impact of the mass media) have made a difference to the way young people see themselves and the way others see them.

In other words, their role has been changed.

One popular image of teenagers would show them as
- Rebellious
- Disrespectful
- Lazy
- Scruffy (or outrageous in their dress)
- Undisciplined
- Sexually immoral

► ► ► ► **TALKING POINT**

- How accurate is this?
- Is it possible to see all young people like this?
- Is there an element of truth in it?

You might find it useful to discuss all these points not from what teenagers are like now but from what has happened in the past.

In other words, see your parents as teenagers. Calculate when they would have been 16 or so and look at the teenage 'cult' which existed then. Can you see them as rebellious and wild youngsters with no respect for their elders, rampaging through life without a thought for anyone else?

If your parents were not in this country at that time or if they were only fairly recent arrivals from another culture, what differences would you expect to find?

This may, in fact, give a clue to the existence in countries like Britain of what is called *youth culture*.

What this means is that young people tend to try to be different from older generations as they try to become more independent.

Much of their effort centres on such things as music and fashion. They may even use a language of their own.

In a way this is a normal part of growing up, but why do many people also see it as a problem?

► ► ► ► **TALKING POINT**

- Why do *you* think this happens?
- Why is it important for young people to feel that they are different and independent?

What follows is a brief explanation of some of the possible reasons for this.

As a child you are very much dependent on adults – they feed and clothe you, look after your welfare and upbringing and try to teach you about the world around you. Your roles in life are limited.

As an adult you are expected to be independent. Now it is your job to look after yourself, have a family of your own. Your roles are many and varied.

Somehow you have to make the change between the two.

But when?

In some societies the change from child to adult is sudden. It may come at a particular age and be recognized through some kind of ceremony. In the Jewish culture this ceremony is called the bar-mitzvah and is only for males.

In Britain and other 'developed' nations this transition is often delayed by economic needs such as education. School keeps people in a dependent role even after they are physically mature enough to be seen as adults in other cultures. (The age of physical and sexual maturity is also gradually getting lower.)

This may lead to problems of *identity* – are you a child or an adult?

Have you ever accused your parents of 'treating you like a kid'?

So young people try to carve out their own identity in a world which may be confused as to how to treat them – yes, the rest of society is as confused as the youngsters about how to deal with this time in our lives.

Below is a chart showing how gradual this change can be.

What is certain is that there are large numbers of companies who are glad of the existence of these 'troublesome' youths. Records, clothes, cosmetics and magazines aimed at the teenage market are big business.

Age	Legal and other rights (or lack of them)
0–5	You are an infant.
10	You become criminally responsible. In other words, you are thought to be able to judge the consequences of your actions and can be held responsible for criminal acts (such as shooting your parents so that you can go to the orphans' tea party!).
13	You can go to work part-time.
14	The law defines you as a 'young person'. You are allowed to go into licensed premises (pub).
16	You are legally allowed to have sexual intercourse. You may marry with your parents' consent. You may leave school and start work full-time. You can buy cigarettes. You can buy beer, wine and perry with a meal on licensed premises. You may ride certain types of motorbike.
17	You may drive a car and more powerful motorbikes.
18	*Bingo!* You've arrived at the 'age of majority'. You can vote, marry, see any film you want to, own property, drink alcohol on licensed premises, gamble, buy goods on credit – in fact, you are a fully fledged adult. (Well, nearly. While you can vote for a particular MP, you cannot become one until you are 21.)

► ► ► ► **TALKING POINT**

- What do you think of these laws?
- Are they reasonable in terms of the ages at which you are allowed to do different things?
- And perhaps more to the point, does the existence of these laws and rules mean that young people *are* more likely to rebel against the rest of society?

One of the most important aspects of this 'youth culture' is the feeling that young people are 'doing their own thing'. No one is telling them what to wear, how to behave, what to think.

The *control* on the group is not from a higher authority such as parents, school or the law. It is the invention of the youngsters themselves and is controlled 'from within' by pressures from groups of like-minded people.

▶ ▶ ▶ ▶ **OR IS IT?**

In 1975/6 a new and outrageous movement burst into life – PUNK.

Many of the older generation were upset by it. These people seemed to have gone too far. Records were banned from the radio, television interviews with the Sex Pistols brought storms of protest.

But it took hold.

Fairly soon there was a move to revive the Mods of the mid-sixties. In the sixties the well-publicized seaside battles between Mods and Rockers had also outraged the older generation, but now they seemed like an acceptable alternative. After all, the Beatles, the Who and the Rolling Stones were by now part of pop legend (they weren't so acceptable in the sixties).

So who decided on this Mod revival? Was it the youngsters themselves, or was it a conspiracy by the older generation to get rid of this menace in their midst?

One observer at the time was quoted as saying that the reason that Punk was unpopular with some people was that it earned little money for the industries which specialized in selling pop culture to young people. After all why should anyone go and spend money on a designer pullover when you could wear a bin liner for about 10p?

Many recent fashions have been strongly based on punk styles so maybe there is some truth in this view.

So who creates the current fashion in music and dress?

▶ ▶ ▶ ▶ **SOMETHING TO DO**

1 In groups discuss the general trends in youth culture at the moment – there are usually a number of different ones which can be identified by a style of music or dress.
2 List the music, clothes and behaviour you associate with each of them.

Then

3 Compare your lists with those of the other groups in the class.
4 Discuss where you think these youth cults came from. Who or what started them off? That is, do young people together dream up an idea which takes hold, or does it all come from a successful band or musical style?
   And how do musical styles become successful?

And then . . . It's *your* turn.

If it really is true that young people invent their own styles it ought to be possible for you to do the same.

In groups again see if you can come up with a completely original style for people of your age group.

1 Describe or even draw the kind of fashion you would like to see
2 What type of music would it be based on?
3 Then discuss your ideas in class

Judging by the reactions you get – and don't be put off by others thinking that it would be ridiculous – discuss whether you think it would be acceptable to other young people (not older generations). That is, what chance is there that it would work?

Remember that Punk did start in this way – as an attempt by some young people to be genuinely different.

▶ ▶ ▶ ▶ THE POINT IS . . .

This kind of exercise is virtually impossible. Would you really wear clothes that were out of fashion now in the hope that you could persuade other people to make them fashionable?

Do you have the power to change things?

- Who does dictate and create fashion?
- What choice do *you* have in the matter?

4

Nice work – if you can get it

By the end of this chapter the student should be able to:
1 Assess the qualities employers look for in employees.
2 Suggest reasons for conflict between management and employees.
3 Recognise the employee's position in the structure of a company.
4 Examine the extent to which the structure of firms shapes industrial relations.

All around the world most people work, or depend on someone else who works in order to live. This work can take many forms, from people who grow their own crops, build their own houses and make their own clothes to those of us in a society like Britain's where work is normally carried out for money which buys what we need in life.

There are many points of view on the way the actual amount people are paid for their work is decided. Some argue that skill should be rewarded, or that the number of people able to do the job should set the wage level – that is, if only a small number of people can do the job then their reward should be higher; if it's a job that just about anyone can do, then the pay should be low.

In 1975 it became law that women should be paid the same as men for doing the same, or an equivalent, job, but how do you compare jobs that may be very different – a bus driver and a school caretaker, for example?

All over the country personnel departments undertake this task when they do what they called *job evaluation*.

▶ ▶ ▶ ▶ **SOMETHING TO DO**

You try it. The chart shows a number of different jobs. Different aspects of the work are listed and you have to give them a score from 1 to 20. For example, if you feel a particular job would be boring, give it a high score under 'boredom' – but bear in mind that the scores apply in relation to each other as well. It's not enough to say that being a dustman may be more boring than being a doctor – you have to try to say *by how much*.

And if you think that a high level of skill is needed then give that job a high score and so on.

Either on your own, or in groups, evaluate the jobs shown section by section, then add up the total scores.

	Airline pilot	Teacher	Bricklayer	Stockbroker	Shop assistant	Nurse	Miner	Bank manager
1 Mental effort								
Qualifications needed	. . . .	. . . .	. . . .	. . . .	. . . .	. . . . .	. . . .	
Intelligence needed at work	. . . .	. . . .	. . . .	. . . .	. . . .	. . . . .	. . . .	
Complexity of job	. . . .	. . . .	. . . .	. . . .	. . . .	. . . . .	. . . .	
Mental stress	. . . .	. . . .	. . . .	. . . .	. . . .	. . . . .	. . . .	
2 Physical effort								
Hard physical work	. . . .	. . . .	. . . .	. . . .	. . . .	. . . . .	. . . .	
Manual skill	. . . .	. . . .	. . . .	. . . .	. . . .	. . . . .	. . . .	
Co-ordination of physical/mental	. . . .	. . . .	. . . .	. . . .	. . . .	. . . . .	. . . .	
3 Danger								
Of illness	. . . .	. . . .	. . . .	. . . .	. . . .	. . . . .	. . . .	
Of accidents	. . . .	. . . .	. . . .	. . . .	. . . .	. . . . .	. . . .	
4 Responsibility								
For safety of others	. . . .	. . . .	. . . .	. . . .	. . . .	. . . . .	. . . .	
For work of others	. . . .	. . . .	. . . .	. . . .	. . . .			. . . .
For money or property and goods	. . . .	. . . .	. . . .	. . . .	. . . .	. . . . .	. . . .	
5 Monotony and repetition	. . . .	. . . .	. . . .	. . . .	. . . .	. . . . .	. . . .	
6 Unsocial aspects, e.g. hours	. . . .	. . . .	. . . .	. . . .	. . . .	. . . . .	. . . .	
Total (out of 280)	. . . .	. . . .	. . . .	. . . .	. . . .	. . . . .	. . . .	

After you have added up the scores for each one:

● Compare your results. Was there much disagreement?
● Discuss the reasons for your scores.
● *By how much* was the lowest score less than the highest score?

Now find out a reasonable average of pay for these jobs. For example, a nurse may earn between £60 and £130 per week.

Is the difference in pay similar to the differences in the scores?

▶ ▶ ▶ ▶   **TALKING POINT**

- Are there any other aspects of work you would want to take into account when assessing jobs?

When this is done in most firms they put a *weighting* on some aspects of the evaluation. This means that the score for 'qualifications' would be multiplied by, say, 3 before the scores were added up, making mental ability more important than danger. Is this fair?

Which of them do *you* think is most important?

In it together?

Unless we work for ourselves, getting and keeping a job involve us in doing what other people want us to do.

This may not always be easy and so it is useful to try to understand some of the different points of view which exist in the work situation.

Example

A firm that employs twenty people may be owned by one person or a small partnership. The views of some of the people who work there may go something like this:

- *Owner*: I've worked damn hard to build up this business. I deserve to be well paid for it. I take all the financial risks and control the whole operation. I am responsible for those people having a job. I am entitled to behave towards them as I see fit for the good of my business.
- *Supervisor*: It's my job to see that the people under my control give of their best. Firms need people like me to keep things going even if I am seen as a bit of a tyrant at times. I have responsibility for the day-to-day running of the firm so that the boss can concentrate on the bigger issues and make sure the firm survives and prospers. Wish I could get on to a management level of pay, though.
- *Assembly worker*: Well, it's a job, and that's something to be grateful for nowadays. Mind you, if I could get a less boring and better-paid job I'd jump at the chance. That supervisor gets on my nerves, doing the boss's dirty work while he goes off and plays golf. Bet he'd pay me more if he had to come down here and do this for eight hours a day, five days a week.

In an industrial society like ours there is a tendency for people to be divided up into a number of specialized areas of work so that even in a small firm you will find people doing a range of different jobs. This may lead to many different points of view about work. It is not just a question of personalities – there is always the possibility of disagreement because what these people see as *important* in a job will depend on what they do and the position they hold in the firm.

▶ ▶ ▶ ▶ **SOMETHING TO DO**

Explore these different viewpoints.

- Start at the beginning and imagine you are going to apply for a job.
- Write down as many things as you can think of that *you* would want from the job.
- Now write down what you think the *employer* will be looking for from you.
- Are there any differences?
- Were any of the things you thought of the same for both?
- Were they in the same order?

Perhaps from this the class can agree on ten things that would make you, in the eyes of an employer, a 'good worker'.

Whether you have these qualities or not it is necessary at some time to convince an employer that you have enough of them for him or her to

- Take you on in the first place.
- Keep you on.

If you manage to work out the kinds of things that will benefit your cause when filling out application forms, you may be invited to an interview. (Sometimes you will go to an interview and be asked to fill out a form when you get there, but the principles are the same.)

The interview game

And game it is.

After all, a game is a contest played under certain rules. The contest here is with other applicants, but it may also seem to be like a war between the interviewer and you – if you don't get it right, that is.

Most interviews go something like this:

1 You go in. Greetings, handshakes, smiles all round. Please sit down.
2 Explanations – who the people are in the room, how long this will take.
3 Confirmations – checking that you are the person they were expecting, where you live, went to school and so on.
4 Questions – why, what do you think of . . . ?
5 *Your* questions.
6 Thank you, goodbye, we'll let you know . . .

The purpose of the interview is not about getting information from you, however. They can do that on the application form and check it with other people who know you, such as your 'referees'.

So what are they looking for?

▶ ▶ ▶ ▶ **SOMETHING TO DO**

Put yourself in the position of those happy, smiling people who are waiting for you to walk into that room. (Well, they will probably be smiling at the beginning, at least.)

Take each of the above stages and try to work out exactly what it is that is happening and what effect this might be having on the person or people interviewing you. What are *they* thinking while you are in that room?

Apart from listening to what you say they are also observing other things about you. What 'clues' are they looking for?

▶ ▶ ▶ ▶ **THE POINT IS . . .**

Remember that you are not only giving information – you are creating an impression. And you have about fifteen minutes in which to do it.

You may see yourself as the best person who ever applied for such a job, but how on earth are you going to let the interviewers know it in such a short time?

▶ ▶ ▶ ▶ **SOMETHING TO DO**

Divide into groups of three or four and imagine that you are the managing committee of a youth club (or the board of directors of a firm – you decide). You are about to appoint a full-time youth leader (or whatever job you decide on).

1 Devise an application form for the job – one you think will give enough information for an interview.
2 Once you have agreed on the form, each of you should fill it in as though you were applying for the job.
3 Examine the applications. Are any of them better than the others? What could be improved to give you a better chance of getting the interview?
4 Now conduct the interviews. The interviewers should devise questions, based on what the applicant has written on the application form, so that each interview is slightly different.
5 Using the applications as a guide, interview each member of the group with the rest of the class as observers.
6 When the interviews are complete, the *observers* should decide on who will get the job and why.

Remember:
● Interviews are designed to gather information, so avoid turning it into a trial.
● Observers should be constructive in their criticisms of both the applicants and the interviewers.
● Applicants should work out for themselves what they think makes a good you leader (or employee in the chosen job) and try to emphasize these qualities themselves when answering questions.

Was there a general level of agreement on who should get the job?

▶ ▶ ▶ ▶ THE POINT IS . . .

In most real job interviews all the applicants could probably do the job. The choice then normally comes down to how well the applicant was able to convince the employer that he or she was better than the others. What the interviewers are doing is trying to imagine each applicant in that particular job and asking themselves, will this person *fit in* with our organization?

So let's assume that you have the job.

Earlier we looked at some of the possible different viewpoints which exist in the workplace.

How do differences of opinion arise?

To understand this it might be helpful to look at the structure of firms.

Business organizations exist to make money. Whoever owns the firm will receive an income out of the profits of the firm. The people who are employed by the firm are paid for their work out of the money the firm receives from selling its products (these can be goods or services).

This means that if wages are very low then the profits will be higher.

So in most cases it is in the interests of the owners of firms to pay the employees as little as possible so that they receive a bigger income themselves.

But people do not like to work for next to nothing. It is in their interests to try to get as much money as possible for the work they do.

Somewhere along the line a compromise is reached and a wage level is set which depends on many things – how easy it is to get workers for that job, whether a trade union exists to represent the employees, what the level of unemployment is, and so on.

And there are other areas of conflict as well, such as whether the working conditions are comfortable, whether the management treat the workers well . . . in fact, all the things likely to affect how much people enjoy their work. Money is certainly important – success may be measured in terms of profit and income by many people – but not everybody works *just* for the money.

▶ ▶ ▶ ▶ TALKING POINT

● What did you see as important in a job in the exercise on page 46?

You may have found that the differences between you and 'the boss' were not just in order of importance but actually in the *types* of things you each are looking for.

There are some areas of common ground, such as wanting the best standard of
~g, through money, you can get for yourself. In this the management and the
in any firm will both want the firm to be successful in order to take the best
wards they can.
an we achieve this?

▶ ▶ ▶ ▶ **SOMETHING TO DO**

First try to list the things you think will make people work hard – and think about it.

If you say 'money', for example, imagine yourself in a job and that the boss has announced that everyone is to have a 50 per cent pay rise. Will this make you work harder?

This whole thing might be easier if you try to think of the things you like about other people's jobs (at least, as far as you know them) or even the things you dislike, or think you would dislike, about jobs you have done or know about.

For example, you may be bored. What is making the job boring and how would you change it to make it more interesting?

Would more variety make you work harder?

(If you are having difficulty thinking up ways to improve work, look at the aspects of jobs in the job evaluation exercise at the beginning of this chapter. This may give you some clues.)

When you have listed your 'grievances' you might like to divide into two groups with one arguing the management viewpoint, giving reasons for *not* changing working methods or conditions and the other arguing for the changes.

A question of safety

▶ ▶ ▶ ▶ **SOMETHING TO DO**

Grievances at work crop up from time to time and may be resolved in many ways.

If the firm is small then it may be possible to sort problems out through informal chats.

In large companies the management are often at a distance from many of the workforce, either physically, by being in separate parts of the building or even in another building, or socially, with a large gap in earnings and responsibilities. Some production workers in large companies will never meet or even see their managing director.

In these situations there is often a formal structure of committees and regular meetings to keep a check on what is happening – in theory a two-way channel of communication between managers and workers.

This may involve such groups as works committees and trade unions.

Before looking at a particular grievance, here are some general points about unions and their role in the workplace.

Trade unions grew out of the Industrial Revolution, a process that made Britain the most powerful nation on earth in the nineteenth century, bringing great wealth to some but harsh and squalid conditions to many others.

It was a time when factory owners had virtual freedom to impose the conditions on their workers – some so harsh that the government was persuaded in 1844, for example, to regulate child labour by making it illegal for children between 9 and 13 to work *more than 68 hours a week*.

After many years of conflict with governments and employers, trade unions won the right to exist and to represent workers in all forms of employment.

Nowadays there are four sorts of union:

1 Craft unions, which represent a particular trade, e.g. electricians.
2 General unions, which represent a range of occupations, mostly unskilled or semi-skilled manual workers, e.g. the Transport and General Workers Union.
3 Industrial unions, which represent workers in a particular industry such as mining and railways, e.g. the National Union of Mineworkers.
4 White-collar unions, representing office and managerial/professional workers, e.g. the National Union of Teachers.

Unions usually make the news only when they are involved in some kind of dispute, such as a strike, but this only happens when both sides have failed to reach an agreement over a particular issue. The instances when management and union come to an agreement across the negotiating table do not make such a dramatic impact and are therefore unheard of except to the parties involved.

But conflicts do happen and to understand why we need to look at the points of view both sides take into their negotiations.

Management aims
- To make the company successful in a competitive market.
- To do this they must keep costs down and profits up.
- This means getting as much work out of the employees as possible for the least cost in wages, equipment, other running costs and wastage.
- This will then produce a product at a low *unit cost* – that is, as much output as possible for a particular level of expense.

Effects of aims
A number of effects result from these aims, many of which are not good news for the employees. In theory they could result in
- Low wages.
- Fewer people employed because machinery is more efficient and, in the long run, cheaper.
- Less interesting jobs for employees. It has long been thought that making each job as simple as possible, such as on a production line, is better for output and profits; but the effect on workers is to make their jobs less skilled and more boring.

Union aims
- To secure the best possible conditions and pay for their members.
- To maintain a high level of employment and job security.
- This means using their *collective* power to uphold the interests of the workforce they represent.
- They hope this will produce higher pay, shorter hours and safer, more comfortable working conditions.

Effects of aims
These aims will have a number of effects that are not good news for the employers. In theory they could result in

- Higher costs.
- Lower productivity – i.e. fewer goods produced at a certain cost than that of a competitor.
- A happier workforce who *may* produce a better product, have fewer days off and stick with the firm.
- They may also reduce a firm's ability to compete and endanger the employees' own jobs.

If left to their own devices it is possible that either side could make a complete mess of things. But it is also true that large numbers of firms survive quite well with efficient management and strong unions, so there must be a point at which compromise and co-operation can work reasonably well.

The following brief 'case study' is fictitious but is the kind of thing that can happen in firms the length and breadth of the country. Study the information given and try to come up with a solution. It can be done in a variety of ways: divide the class into union and management and argue the case with a third group acting as observers; discuss both sides in small groups and present your conclusions to the rest of the class, then come up with a solution; or simply discuss the whole case as a class.

The company

Grind and Graunch is a company that makes gearbox parts for the major motor manufacturers and car service companies in Great Britain. They produce their parts from an old factory in a small town in the Midlands and are owned by Mr Norman Grind and Mr Bertram Graunch, the founders, who are now in semi-retirement. They leave the day-to-day running of the firm to Bill Travers, the works manager, and Graham Thorn, the production manager. It is an old engineering company in which investment has been low in recent years and in which Travers and Thorn have had problems in implementing new ideas because of the traditional attitudes of the owners.

It employs

- 35 production workers – 27 skilled machinists and 8 labourers
- 3 supervisors
- a chief engineer
- 12 others such as canteen staff, stores supervisor and maintenance workers

The management and staff, apart from Thorn and Travers, comprise an accountant, an administration and personnel manager and 3 secretaries.

The situation

On the morning of 7 February the firm was visited by a factory inspector from the Health and Safety Executive who inspected the machine shop. He found a number of minor problems, such as an excess of waste on the floor between machines and a leaking roof that was letting water run down the walls dangerously close to an electrical junction box.

The main criticism in his report, however, was of the general condition of the machinery. Two lathes and a milling machine were found to have faulty safety cut-outs and he put a prohibition notice on them immediately. This meant that they were out of service until repaired, leaving three of the production workers without work for the two days it took to obtain the parts and replace them.

The following week, when the pay packets came round, the three workers who had been left without machines to work on found they had lost two days' bonus payments. They immediately contacted Peter Smith, their shop steward, who took the matter to Mrs Anne Evans, the administration and personnel manager. She insisted that under company rules people could not be paid for work they had not done but would explain the situation to Mr Travers. Smith was not satisfied the matter would be sorted out quickly and so he asked for a meeting with the management the next day. He also asked that both Mr Thorn and Mr Travers be there to discuss the wider issue of equipment safety. Mr Smith also asked for two workers' representatives from the works committee to be allowed to attend.

The agenda for the emergency meeting was thus set as:

1. Equipment safety and replacement.
2. Bonus payments.

The people

Peter Smith: Has worked at Grind and Graunch for 12 years. A skilled lathe operator, he has been shop steward for 5 years as the local representative for the Amalgamated Engineering Union and now spends most of his time on union duties as agreed with the management. He has long been concerned at the lack of investment in new machinery and in the general condition of the factory. He is aware that the firm needs to move with the times but is worried that the management will see this as an opportunity to cut the workforce.

Bill Travers: An engineer by training, he has been works manager for 7 years. He would like to see the firm become more competitive although he does not feel that this is an urgent problem because the product is of high quality and the firm has a very good reputation with its customers for excellent workmanship and reliable delivery. He sometimes feels his life would be easier if he had a freer hand with spending, especially since getting approval for change from the owners is a slow process.

Graham Thorn: Production manager for the last 3 years having worked his way up from apprentice, he is proud of his record for increasing output over that time. Dislikes unions in general and Peter Smith in particular, feeling that with less interference from the shop floor he could make production much more efficient. He feels that too many people are employed to do the work as it is and would like to see more computer-controlled equipment to improve productivity.

Anne Evans: Personnel manager for only 8 months, she has some sympathy for the workforce. Everything in the firm is old-fashioned, including the office systems she has to work with, and she would like to see more spending on anything that will improve efficiency. Is aware of the good labour relations record in the firm and knows the employees are generally happy and loyal. Sees this job as a stepping stone to better things and is therefore reluctant to upset anyone, particularly Thorn and Travers.

The meeting

What actually happens is up to you, as is the decision you reach, but here are some general points:

1 Investment in new machinery has a number of advantages – higher productivity and therefore higher wages and profits. It will solve many of the safety problems. But at what level of spending and with what effect on the size of the workforce? Is the market big enough to take an increase in output, or should the firm aim to keep the same market with a smaller workforce?

There have been seven reported safety problems with machines in the last 3 months. Nobody wants to see any serious injuries or the firm being fined.

What action can management take? Bill Travers would not want to impose a settlement and Peter Smith would not want to have to ask for industrial action – they both know that the motor industry is not above switching suppliers at a moment's notice.

2 Bonus payments are calculated on a standard level of output for each machinist. Anything above this – and the machine shop is always above this level – is paid at an agreed bonus rate. It depends of course on the machines being in action. Bonus is always reduced if a machine breaks down, but these stoppages are usually short. However, they have been occurring more often just lately.

The three workers are claiming that their loss of bonus was not their fault and are asking that their average bonus for the last month be paid for this week.

Both Travers and Thorn receive a 6-monthly payment linked to output – a kind of management bonus.

3 Some figures: a replacement machine for each of the operations in the machine shop will average out at £30,000 but would increase productivity by up to 50 per cent. It would be necessary to buy twelve machines to replace what they have now and this would result in a loss of ten jobs if it was done all at once. It would also mean re-negotiating the bonus package but would probably result in higher earnings for those kept on. The machines would pay for themselves in 18 months to 2 years.

Try to come to an agreement which is acceptable to all parties. Refer back to the general aims of management and unions on page 50 to help you to understand the viewpoints if necessary.

When you have reached agreement, write a report to Mr Grind and Mr Graunch explaining what you want done and why. They are the ones who will have to come up with the money.

5

Behave yourself

By the end of this chapter the student should be able to:
1 Assess the need for rules and regulations.
2 Examine the ways in which rules may apply unequally to various groups in society.
3 Assess the extent to which authority and power are used responsibly.
4 Suggest ways in which rules may be used to change behaviour.
5 Evaluate the methods of ensuring adherence to rules.

We saw in Chapter 3 that young people may have problems which are brought about by the law – what you are or are not allowed to do at certain ages. But restrictions apply to all of us.

▶ ▶ ▶ ▶ **SOMETHING TO DO**

The following chart shows the hours of the day. Fill in brief details of what you might be doing at the times shown, what regulations apply and who makes the rule (authority).

You don't have to think in terms of law-breaking or major crimes because just travelling to school, college or work involves you in bye-laws, such as having to pay your fare on the bus. Driving a car makes you subject to criminal law. Schools, colleges, work-places all have their own written and unwritten rules.

Of course, there are rules that apply all the time and wherever you are, and they stop most of us from committing such crimes as murder and theft. But we also forget that many daily activities we take as normal behaviour are governed by many laws.

For example, if you go into a shop to buy a record both you and the retailer are subject to such laws as the Sale of Goods Act, the Trades Descriptions Act, the law on contract. Moreover the retailer is required to collect VAT and is legally bound to hand it over to Customs and Excise, and is also required to keep accurate records of transactions, and so on . . .

When you have made out your list, discuss it with the rest of the class to see what you included or left out.

Time	Activity	Rule/regulation	Authority
7.00– 8.00	. . . .	. . . .	. . . .
8.00– 9.00	. . . .	. . . .	. . . .
9.00–10.00	. . . .	. . . .	. . . .
10.00–11.00	. . . .	. . . .	. . . .
11.00–12.00	. . . .	. . . .	. . . .
12.00– 1.00	. . . .	. . . .	. . . .
1.00– 2.00	. . . .	. . . .	. . . .
2.00– 3.00	. . . .	. . . .	. . . .
3.00– 4.00	. . . .	. . . .	. . . .
4.00– 5.00	. . . .	. . . .	. . . .
5.00– 6.00	. . . .	. . . .	. . . .
6.00– 7.00	. . . .	. . . .	. . . .
7.00– 8.00	. . . .	. . . .	. . . .
8.00– 9.00	. . . .	. . . .	. . . .
9.00–10.00	. . . .	. . . .	. . . .
10.00–11.00	. . . .	. . . .	. . . .
11.00–12.00	. . . .	. . . .	. . . .

Did you find it difficult to work out the 'rules' for the time you were at home? There are many more than just what your family expects from you . . .

▶ ▶ ▶ ▶ **THE POINT IS . . .**

We are governed by a vast number of rules all the time and it is to our credit that we actually know what they are because ignorance is no defence in law. This means that if you did not know you were doing wrong you cannot use this as an excuse.

All societies have laws, from small tribal groups, where control is exercised by a few senior individuals, to complex societies like ours, which have large and complicated legal systems needing specialists to help us understand their laws.

But why are so many laws passed? What are they there for?

The reason for some laws seems obvious – crimes like murder, theft, assault and rape are *anti-social* activities where we might say that there is a *moral* basis to the need to prevent them.

But the laws of some societies do not always apply elsewhere. For instance, in Muslim countries alcoholic drink is generally illegal while it is a very well accepted part of life in other parts of the world.

It is beyond the scope of this book to examine the details of how laws are made but it would be useful to think of *why* they are made, *who* benefits from them and *how* they are enforced.

▶ ▶ ▶ ▶ **SOMETHING TO DO**

Using a grid like the one below and working in small groups, think of about four or five rules and regulations you dislike or find difficult to accept. Then fill in the columns so that you have some notes for discussing them as a class.

For example:

Rule: Radios or cassette players not allowed on school/college premises.
Who made it? Head teacher/Principal.
Who is meant to benefit? Everyone from a lack of noise and less likelihood of awkward losses or thefts.
What problems can it cause? Unhappy students who like to listen to music.
Who enforces it? All the teaching staff.
What is the punishment? Confiscation for that day, worse if repeated.
Is there room for negotiation? (That is, are there any times when the rule can be relaxed or suspended?) No.
How would you change it? Abolish the rule perhaps, or modify it to allow personal stereos with headphones.
What would happen if you did? Does not get rid of theft problem and students may attempt to listen during classes but noise level problem is eliminated.

	Rule 1	Rule 2	Rule 3	Rule 4	Rule 5
Who made it?					
Who is meant to benefit?					
What problems can it cause?					
Who enforces it?					
What is the punishment?					
Is there room for negotiation?					
How would you change it?					
What would happen if you did?					

While we may find some laws a bit of a nuisance it is a fact that the vast majority of us obey most of them most of the time. Even bad drivers usually stay on the left side of the road, for example.

But why do we obey?

Obviously, driving on the left in Britain is sensible because everyone else does it – it is safer for the individual and we can therefore see some benefit from it.

But there are some laws that people dislike. They may still obey them but would rather not; and there is some evidence to suggest that if there is no one around, such as the police, to make us obey then we would not all 'behave ourselves'.

On the other hand, in America in the 1920s a law was passed which banned all alcoholic drink – this became known as Prohibition. It led to even worse problems for the authorities when gangs of criminals defied the government and ran illegal drinking clubs.

▶ ▶ ▶ ▶ **TALKING POINT**

- So does this mean that an unpopular law is unlikely to work? Prohibition eventually failed.
- And is it okay to break a 'bad' law?

▶ ▶ ▶ ▶ **SOMETHING TO DO**

Perhaps you can find out what other people's attitudes are to breaking the rules.

Ask people in your school or college the following questions and then draw up a table or chart of the answers.

---

1 Age

2 Sex M ☐ F ☐

3 Do you think of yourself as law-abiding? i.e. do you follow the rules
Always ☐ Most of the time ☐ Sometimes ☐ Hardly ever ☐ Never ☐

4 Do you think you could commit a serious crime?
Yes ☐ No ☐ Maybe ☐
(If Yes, answer question 5; if No or Maybe, answer question 6.)

5 What is the most serious crime you think you could commit?
....

6 What would stop you?
Fear of being caught ☐ Fear of being punished severely ☐
The shame of being thought a criminal ☐
You think it is wrong to break the law ☐

7 If you knew that nothing could happen to you, which of the following crimes do you think you *could* commit?
Murder ☐ Armed robbery ☐ Burglary ☐ Theft from a person ☐
Shoplifting ☐ Arson ☐ Car theft ☐ Handling stolen goods ☐
Drunk driving ☐ Speeding ☐ None ☐

Continued

8 Do you think that sentences handed out by courts are usually
Too heavy ☐ About right ☐ Too light? ☐

9 Are there any crimes you think are *always* dealt with too lightly?
Yes ☐ (If so, state which ....)
No ☐

10 Do you think that more severe punishment would stop a lot of crime
nowadays?
Yes ☐ No ☐ Don't know ☐

What conclusions did you come to? In particular:

- Were there any *types* of crimes people would be more likely to commit if they knew nothing could happen to them?
- Why do you think this is?
- Would people be more likely to commit crimes if there was no control or authority to stop them?
- Did the *seriousness* of the crime make any difference?

► ► ► ► **THE POINT IS . . .**

Studies have shown that the level of control is usually more important than moral principles in preventing criminal acts.

But . . .

How do we define 'a crime'?

In the earlier exercise on rules and who makes them you were asked to think about who benefits from certain rules or regulations.

When thinking about the 'law of the land', is it true to say that all laws are made for the benefit of the whole society?

It seems obvious that murder should be seen as a crime, but we are allowed to kill people if we put on a uniform and are told to kill to defend our country.

Taking heroin is illegal. But not all drugs are condemned by everybody. Some people believe that taking cannabis is less harmful than drinking alcohol or smoking cigarettes, yet it is illegal in Britain. (There is a more detailed look at drugs in Chapter 7.)

Perhaps the easiest way to examine law-making is to give you the chance to do it yourself. But you will have to work for it.

► ► ► ► **SOMETHING TO DO**

Play the following game.

It goes something like this:

- You will need counters (or something similar) of five different colours – enough for each person in the class to have five each. (A table showing how many of each for the number of players is shown below.)

- You start by drawing the counters one by one out of a bag without looking at them. Go round the class until you each have five.
- Then you add up the score you have in your hand.
- Points are scored as follows (these are only suggested colours):

Gold   – 25 pts
Red   – 20 pts
Green – 15 pts
White – 10 pts
Blue   – 5 pts

- In addition you score bonuses as follows:

  3 counters of one colour – double the score in your hand
  4   „   „   „   „   – treble the score in your hand
  5   „   „   „   „   – quadruple the score in your hand

Thus a hand of 1 red, 3 green and 1 white is $20 + 45 + 10 = 75$ + bonus (75×2) $= 150$

The first thing to do is simply to add up the score and tell your teacher who will write it down on a score sheet.

Ready reckoner for ratio of counters to go into the bag

Number of players	Number of counters					
	Gold	**Red**	**Green**	**White**	**Blue**	**Total**
10	3	6	10	14	17	50
11	3	7	11	15	19	55
12	4	8	12	16	20	60
13	4	8	13	17	23	65
14	4	9	14	19	24	70
15	5	10	15	20	25	75
16	5	10	16	21	28	80
17	5	11	17	23	29	85
18	6	12	18	24	30	90
19	6	12	19	26	32	95
20*	6	13	20	27	34	100

* For numbers over 20 simply add together the relevant numbers 10–20.

Score sheet

Player's name /	Round 1	Round 2	Round 3	Round 4	Round 5	Round 6
. . . .	. . . .	. . . .	. . . .	. . . .	. . . .	. . . .
. . . .	. . . .	. . . .	. . . .	. . . .	. . . .	. . . .
. . . .	. . . .	. . . .	. . . .	. . . .	. . . .	. . . .
. . . .	. . . .	. . . .	. . . .	. . . .	. . . .	. . . .

etc.

Now all you have to do is play the game.

Obviously it would be pointless for everyone to stay with the score you have, so you can try to improve it. This is done by trading.

Do not show anyone else your counters. If you want to trade you should show this by sitting with your hands on your lap. You will need to move around to make the trade with someone else which you do by *linking arms*.

Once you have done this you *must* trade counters.

If you are happy with your score and do not want to trade, you must sit with your arms folded.

You will notice that it is possible to improve your score by giving away higher scoring counters for lower if this helps with the bonus points.

For this first round you are allowed 2 minutes.

Then you must work out your score and tell your teacher who will make a note of it on the sheet.

Now repeat the first round of trading and give your teacher the scores.

At this point the teacher will divide the class into three groups. They ought to be of roughly equal size but they must be based on the scores.

Group A will be the group with the highest scores, group B the next and group C the third of the class with the lowest scores.

So that the groups can be easily identified it would be useful to have coloured badges or armbands to wear.

Once the class is divided into three, group A is allowed to make up another rule for the game. At this stage the teacher has the right to disallow the rule if it is too extreme in which case they must make up another rule.

Then another round is played.

The scores are given in and anyone who has enough to get into group A will be allowed to do so. Also, if a group member has lost points he/she can be relegated to the next group down.

Group A can now make another rule provided it keeps the game going.

Then another round with up and down movements still based on scores.

Then the next rule from group A.

And so on . . .

Keep going for as long as the game can stand it (you'll see what I mean as it unfolds before you).

Two final points:

● Group A make the rules
● The winners are the people in group A when the game ends.

Postscript

When the game finishes discuss how you felt about it, answering the following questions

● Was the game fair?
● Who enjoyed it?
● Does what happened bear any relation to the 'real world'?
● Has the game answered any questions about rule-making?
● What other issues has it raised?

▶ ▶ ▶ ▶   **THE POINT IS . . .**

- Rules have a job to do in society.
- They are there to provide a structure in which people can live their lives knowing that certain behaviour is or isn't allowed.
- They also need to be *enforced*.

You may have found in the game, as in many other games, that people who are not winning tend to give up or complain about the rules being unfair. If we all did this all the time then there would be no 'order', but it is not easy to leave the 'game' when we are talking about living our daily lives.

In Britain most people believe that the laws are generally fair and apply to everyone equally – although there are some groups who would disagree.

▶ ▶ ▶ ▶   **TALKING POINT**

In some countries such as South Africa the laws are written quite obviously in the interests of a particular, powerful group of people. While black people there may not like the rules they are required not to break them and risk severe punishments if they want to see any changes take place.

But in Britain, where more opinions and sections of society are represented in Parliament (where the laws are made), we tend to see change in the law as something that is possible to achieve.

BUT . . .

Does this mean that when we change the way people are allowed to behave we also change their *attitudes*?

For example, it is illegal in Britain to discriminate against people on the grounds of their race, colour, religion or sex. Does this also mean that we will eventually stop *wanting* to discriminate in this way?

Can changing a law change people's attitudes as well as their behaviour?

How would you go about changing someone's mind by changing the rules?

In Chapter 3 we looked at young people in relation to some of the laws that affect them, so here is . . .

▶ ▶ ▶ ▶   **SOMETHING TO DO**

You may have thought that the laws were a little confusing so here's your chance to express your ideas on what you would do to change them.

Your *aim* must be to simplify the rules for young people while making it possible for older people to accept that youngsters are responsible enough to handle them.

You should also bear in mind that change normally happens gradually because it takes people time to adjust. (Women's rights, for example, has been an issue in politics for more than a hundred years and it is still facing a lot of opposition.)

Taking punishment

A number of years ago a young black man was convicted of raping a white woman in Alabama in the United States. He was sentenced to 1,500 years in prison because, as the judge said at the time, 500 years would have been just a 'slap on the wrist'.

If we are to enforce the law it is usually necessary to find some way of punishing people if they break the rules.

But how do we set a punishment that fits the crime?

First we have to decide what we are trying to achieve when we deal with offenders.

There are four main viewpoints which apply to this situation.

1 *Revenge* – the idea that society can somehow 'get its own back' on the offender.
2 *Prevention* or *deterrence* – making the punishment severe enough to stop people taking the risk of being caught.
3 *Retribution* – making the offender pay back a debt to society by making good.
4 *Reform* – trying to make the offender see the error of his or her ways, 'see the light' and not do it again.

All of these approaches have been used at some time or another to deal with criminals, but there are problems with all of them:

- Hanging murderers (revenge) has often resulted in the wrong person being executed.
- Hanging people for stealing sheep was abolished when it was realised that the thief was also killing the shepherd – if the punishment is very severe it may encourage people to commit more serious crimes since nothing worse can happen to them if they are caught.
- How do you work out what is the right level of 're-payment' to victims of crime? How can a rapist 'make it up' to a victim who may be mentally scarred for life?
- Reform is seen by persistent criminals as a waste of time and may even encourage them to carry on since they see the 'punishment' as soft and worth the risk.

In practice there is an element of all these things in most forms of punishment which are handed down to offenders.

Could *you* make the punishment fit the crime?

You don't even need to know the law to pass sentences on people – being a magistrate in Britain is just a question of being accepted as a responsible enough person to be able to decide on cases. Serious crimes, though, are dealt with by crown courts where qualified judges sit, but a magistrate usually hears the case first.

Magistrates who are not legally qualified sit as teams of three and give judgment about guilt or innocence and then pass sentence.

How would *you* get on?

▶ ▶ ▶ ▶ SOMETHING TO DO

In groups acting as magistrates, give your judgement on the following cases and then explain your reasons for your actions. When you have decided on the case it is usual to take the circumstances of the case into account before passing sentence. In every case you can decide on the guilt or otherwise of the defendant and your options are listed under each case. If you want to pass a more severe sentence you must pass the case on to a crown court for sentencing.

1. Mrs Betty Smith was caught leaving a supermarket with a small tin of salmon in her handbag after paying for a number of other items. She was arrested by the store detective.

In court she was too distressed to say much on her own behalf but her solicitor explained that she was 67 and very poor, living in squalid conditions in a privately rented flat. Most of her money that week had gone on heating bills and she took the salmon to supplement her rather poor diet.

She has no family living nearby who can help or even want to. She fully admits to her offence and is sincerely sorry. She has no previous criminal record.

Your options

- An absolute discharge – i.e. the case is dismissed with no further action against Mrs Smith.
- A conditional discharge – no action now but she would be liable to a further sentence if she repeated the offence (on top of any sentence for the next offence).
- A fine up to £1,000.
- A prison sentence – up to 6 months which can be suspended for up to 2 years or a combination of both.
- In addition you can recommend probation, reports and an investigation by the Social Services Department into her circumstances.

2. Both of these cases arose from the same event.

(a) Peter Jones (19) is a student at a nearby college and was on a demonstration against a visit to Britain by a South African minister. There were a number of scuffles in the crowd and when the police went in to restore calm, Jones was arrested for assaulting a police officer.

The police constable's version of the story was that he had gone into the crowd to arrest a demonstrator whom he had seen throw a flour bomb when he was grabbed from behind by Jones and pushed to the ground.

Jones's version was that the police officer pushed past him and grabbed a friend of his, presumably to arrest him for throwing the flour bomb since he heard the officer say, 'I saw that son. You're nicked.' Jones had tapped the officer on the shoulder to tell him that the flour bomb had been thrown by someone else, when the crowd surged and they all stumbled. He denied wrestling the officer to the ground.

Jones has no previous convictions.

(b) Albert Hoskins (38) was arrested at the demonstration for behaviour likely to occasion a breach of the peace and affray. He was one of a group of counter-demonstrators from the local National Front who had turned up to lend their support to the South African minister.

A police constable gave evidence that Hoskins had been chanting obscenities at the main demonstration and later broke through police lines to attack a student who had returned the verbal abuse. While no one was badly hurt in the incident it took two police officers to restrain Hoskins who was extremely agitated.

In his defence Hoskins accepted that he had perhaps lost his temper but was severely provoked by the tone of language used against him by a group of the demonstrators nearest to him. He denies both charges, feeling that he was 'set up' by the students' taunts. He apologized for losing his temper.

Hoskins has three previous convictions for assault, one for affray and two for being drunk and disorderly.

Your options
- Absolute discharge – i.e. acquit them of any offence.
- Conditional discharge.
- A fine – up to £1,000.
- Imprisonment – up to 6 months which can be suspended for up to 2 years.
- A combination of both.
- Probation and reports.
- In addition the offender can be bound over to keep the peace in the sum of . . . i.e. if they are convicted of assault or a similar offence again, the sum becomes payable as an automatic fine.

   (This is slightly unreal since previous convictions would only come to the court's attention if the suspect was found guilty. This is then used to help set the sentence.)

3. James Allen (31) is accused of inflicting grievous bodily harm on William Caxton (40) following an incident in which Caxton claims to have been nearly run over.

Caxton said that he was crossing the road at a T-junction when Allen's van came round the corner at great speed and nearly ran him over. Caxton shouted at the van as it drove on, angered by what he saw as reckless driving. Then the van stopped and Allen got out and approached Caxton angrily. When Caxton repeated his view that Allen was driving recklessly, Allen head-butted him then kicked him repeatedly as he lay on the ground. A passer-by rang for an ambulance in a local shop after taking Allen's registration number as he sped away. The passer-by did not see the actual incident, only Allen leaving Caxton lying in the road. Caxton sustained a broken nose and cracked ribs.

Allen claimed that Caxton had struck the first blow following the argument. He stopped because Caxton had been abusive to him for no apparent reason and had gone back to find out what had upset him. He apologized for the ferocity of the attack but felt he was severely provoked. He had also been under some stress at work recently and had had a bad day.

Allen has three previous convictions for motoring offences and one for affray.

Your options
As in the previous case.

4. Randolph Irwin (17) was on board a Boeing 747 en route from Jerusalem to New York. It had just taken off from London Heathrow after a refuelling stop when Irwin, by his own admission, decided to play a prank with his friends. They were members of a theological college who had just finished a three-week visit to the Holy Land and were becoming bored with the flight. They started writing down and passing messages among themselves, then Irwin wrote the message, 'There is a bomb on board,' and passed it to a stewardess, claiming to have found it in the toilet. The stewardess took the message to the captain who made an emergency landing at Manchester airport after dumping the plane's load of fuel and alerting the emergency services on the ground. Irwin's solicitor told the court that Irwin was very sorry for what he had done, not realizing the likely consequences of his actions. The court was also told that Irwin was a model student who soon hoped to graduate and train as a priest in the Catholic Church.

The court also heard that the cost of the dumped fuel was £9,000 and the cost of alerting the emergency services and foaming the runway was £3,500.

Your options

As in case 2.

Make a note of your decisions and discuss them in class.

- Did you find that any of your prejudices came into play when you were deciding on sentences?
- Did you find yourself judging the defendants as to how 'bad' you thought they were as people, or did you genuinely try to judge each case purely on its merits?
- Did you feel that the options open to you were limited?

Would you like to be a magistrate? Because you can if you want to provided you are seen as a responsible enough person for the job.

And in case you were wondering, these are actual cases. The names have been changed and the information summarized, but they are essentially what happened.

In case 1, Betty Smith was given an absolute discharge. Given her circumstances the magistrate thought that there was no chance of her doing the same again and they felt that she had suffered enough with the shame, as she saw it, of the case being brought. In other words, they felt that her 'offence' was almost understandable in the situation she was in.

In case 2, Peter Jones was fined £150. Albert Hoskins was fined £100 and bound over to keep the peace in the sum of a further £100.

In case 3, James Allen was fined £100.

In case 4, Randolph Irwin was sent to prison for 3 months.

6

I wanna tell you a story

By the end of this chapter the student should be able to:

1 Recognise the extent to which persuasion is used by the various mass communications media.
2 Assess the methods used to achieve this.
3 Recognise the part played by mass communications in socialisation.
4 Assess the role of the media in attitude formation and reinforcement.
5 Examine the extent to which he/she is influenced by the media.

How much do you know about these people, things and events? (tick the right column)

	Expert	Above average	About average	Know a little	Hardly anything/ nothing
Your family	......	....	....	....	....
Your school/college	......	....	....	....	....
Terry Wogan	......	....	....	....	....
Terry Waite	......	....	....	....	....
Kenny Dalglish	......	....	....	....	....
Nigel Lawson	......	....	....	....	....
$E = mc^2$	......	....	....	....	....
AIDS	......	....	....	....	....
Cars	......	....	....	....	....
The Russian Revolution	......	....	....	....	....
Bricklaying	......	....	....	....	....
Income tax	......	....	....	....	....
Cooking	......	....	....	....	....
The Royal Family	......	....	....	....	....
Buying a house	......	....	....	....	....
Gardening	......	....	....	....	....
The United States	......	....	....	....	....
Your home town	......	....	....	....	....
Nuclear energy	......	....	....	....	....

Computers	. . . . . .	. . . .	. . . .	. . . .	. . . .
Trade unions	. . . . . .	. . . .	. . . .	. . . .	. . . .
Heroin	. . . . . .	. . . .	. . . .	. . . .	. . . .
The Pope	. . . . . .	. . . .	. . . .	. . . .	. . . .

How did you do?

You may have guessed that this was not a test of what you know.

Now go back over it and write in *where* you got your information from – at least for those where you claim to be an expert, know more than the 'average person', or even know 'about average' on the subject.

▶ ▶ ▶ ▶ THE POINT IS . . .

If we know a lot about something it is probably because we become *personally* involved in it or *take the trouble to find out* more than other people.

How often did you find that what you know comes from watching telelvision? Or reading newspapers?

Did anyone claim to be an expert on something and also claim to have got the information from TV?

And what kinds of things did you know virtually nothing about?

Oh, by the way. How many of you thought that $E = mc^2$ was a rock song rather than an important part of Einstein's theory of relativity? Not that it matters too much – we all use the information that we think is important.

▶ ▶ ▶ ▶ FACT

Just about every home in Britain has a television.

And we spend a lot of time watching it.

The figure below shows how much television we watch on average.

Television viewing: by social class and sex

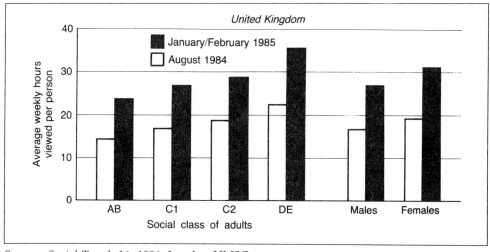

Source: *Social Trends* 16, 1986, London HMSO.

▶ ▶ ▶ ▶ **SOMETHING TO DO**

1 Suggest reasons for:
   (a) The fact that different age groups spend different amounts of time watching TV (see page 79).
   (b) The differences between social classes in their viewing habits.

2 What would you expect to be the differences in the *types* of programmes watched by the different groups?
3 Describe what you think home and family life would be like if we didn't have television.

▶ ▶ ▶ ▶ **FACT**

On 1 February 1987, a Sunday, the four television channels between them put on 65 hours and 5 minutes of programmes.
Of this there were:

- 5 hours 40 minutes of news and current affairs.
- 4 hours 45 minutes of arts programmes.
- 6 hours 5 minutes of films.
- 9 hours 5 minutes of sport.
- There were also many hours of 'educational' programmes, ranging from the Open University to wildlife documentaries and 'factual' programmes.

Virtually none of these programmes was on during peak viewing time in the evening. So what was?

What is your impression of the types of programme most commonly shown on television?

The media

Or, more accurately, the media of mass communication, are relatively modern developments. They include

- Television
- Newspapers
- Radio
- Cinema (or, more commonly now, video films)
- Advertising

Their aims are to

- Inform
- Educate
- Entertain
- Persuade

We shall be concentrating on two of these – information and persuasion.

The following article by Sarah Bond appeared in the *Daily Express* of 31 January 1987.

Princess Anne becomes the first Royal to appear in a TV quiz show on Thursday when she gamely tackles *A Question of Sport* (BBC1, 8.25 pm) on Emlyn Hughes' team.

'She was a super contestant,' enthuses Emlyn, 'and she answered questions on lots of sports – not just ones about horses and riding. She was very relaxed and seemed to enjoy every minute.'

Apart from proving her prowess, the Princess was rewarded with three *Question of Sport* sweaters for herself and her two children, Peter and Zara.

They will be eager to see how their mother fares alongside fellow guests Scottish Rugby union star John Rutherford, athlete Linford Christie and racing driver Nigel Mansell.

The BBC is doggedly keeping mum about the outcome – swearing even the studio audience to secrecy.

A perfectly normal, everyday article. But even this is not just factual. It contains a number of statements and words that give us a clue to how the writer feels about royalty and how she wants us to react as well. Perhaps you can find them for yourself, but here is an alternative article about the same programme which may give you some clues.

European 100 metres champion Linford Christie becomes only the fifth black athlete to appear on a TV quiz show when he tears through *Question of Sport* on BBC 1 this week.

'He was a super contestant,' enthused Emlyn Hughes, his team captain in the show. 'He answered questions on other sports as well as athletics and was great fun to have on the team.'

He will be rewarded with a *Question of Sport* sweater which he promised to wear when he sits down to watch the recording with his family who are eager to know how he fared.

The BBC are not letting on who won the quiz which also included John Rutherford, Scottish Rugby player, Nigel Mansell, racing driver and Princess Anne, former European three-day event champion.

Nudist Leap-frog Club – Vicar Tells All

▶ ▶ ▶ ▶ **SOMETHING TO DO**

Here are some facts. On their own they would make pretty boring reading. Can you spice them up a bit, adding your own interpretations and viewpoint – in as subtle a way as possible, of course. Just imagine that you are a reporter on the same paper as the photographer in the story and you are called along when he rings you about an incident.

Billy Strangelove is a singer with a rock band.

The band is called 'The Nurds'.

Billy is 28.

He is married with two children.

The Nurds' latest record, 'Doombrain' is currently No. 3 in the charts.

He was seen in an Indian restaurant last night with a woman.

Her name is Glenys Drab, but she uses the name Anastasia in her career as a fashion model.

She is 19.

A photographer in the restaurant took their picture as they ate.

The photographer is 39.

Billy became upset.

He swore at the photographer.

The photographer works for a daily newspaper and was having a meal after a heavy night's drinking which he started after finishing work.

The photographer laughed and took another picture.

Billy became more upset and went over to the photographer to ask him to stop taking pictures.

The photographer swore at Billy.

A fight started.

The photographer received a cut eye.

The restaurant owner called the police.

The restaurant owner is 53.

Write the story as you see it.

And don't forget the *headline*.

Then compare your stories. Did you find that there was any common theme or style that cropped up regularly? Perhaps you wrote it in the style of one of the tabloids such as the *Sun* or the *Daily Mirror*. If you did, this would not be surprising – not necessarily because you read these papers but because this is the kind of story they would print. It may just be possible that we are influenced by *what* the papers decide to tell us as much as *how* they tell us.

We in Britain are among the most regular newspaper readers of any country in the world. But does quantity say anything about quality? At the moment we have the following national daily newspapers available in Britain:

	Circulation
Sun	4,061,781
Daily Mirror	3,048,963
Star	1,421,085
Today	350,000 (approx.)
Daily Mail	1,801,317
Daily Express	1,855,627
Daily Telegraph	1,156,304
Guardian	524,264
Times	471,483
Financial Times	251,554
Independent	250,000 (approx.)

There are also Sunday newspapers which are owned by the same companies that own these.

And they all have a particular point of view. This is because they are owned by powerful corporations or individuals, and while we might like to believe that television is run on the lines of providing a balanced view of the world, there is no such restriction on newspapers. Newspapers like the *Guardian* and the *Independent* may well try to give a balanced view of events but they still appeal to a particular kind of reader.

▶ ▶ ▶ ▶ TALKING POINT

If you look at the circulation figures you may notice that the so-called 'quality' papers have the lowest sales. What does this say about our tastes?

Have the tabloids really got it right – churning out a very simple and immediate style of paper that is easy to read but which doesn't demand too much of the reader?

In short, do we have the papers we deserve?

▶ ▶ ▶ ▶ SOMETHING TO DO

Look at the papers mentioned above and examine:

- The language used in the stories.
- The types of stories they carry.
- The *balance* of the content (e.g. sport, news, scandal, etc.).
- The types of features carried in some papers which do not appear in others (e.g. the court circular in the *Daily Telegraph*; horoscopes in the tabloids).

It may be easier if you divide into groups and take one or two papers each, then present your findings to the rest of the class.

Apart from the *content* of newspapers there is also *style* to be considered. The *language* used by papers may be

- Factual
- Emotive
- Sensational

'Factual' is what it says – it just gives accurate information.

'Emotive' is a style which is asking you to feel a particular way about something – outraged, happy, sad, amused, etc.

'Sensational' is a form of exaggeration of an incident which gives it greater importance than it deserves – using the front page to tell of a rock star's love affair when a war has just broken out somewhere in the world.

▶ ▶ ▶ ▶ **SOMETHING TO DO**

Here are some examples of headlines taken from various papers. Can you put them into these categories?

- BIG MAC TO AXE KENT'S LEFTIE PITS
- TRAGEDY OF THE LATCH-KEY KIDS
- EASTENDERS STARS TOLD TO BEHAVE
- THREE DIE IN PLANE CRASH
- BARMY BERNIE IN WITCH HUNT OVER DEMO
- TURKEY SHOOT! ENGLAND COAST IT
- BRIGHTON BOMBING – FOUR HELD
- UNDER 16s CAN HAVE PILL
- PILL MUM IN BUST-UP: I'll Be Back Says Brave Victoria
- SEX OFFENDERS – A NEW APPROACH
- ENGLAND MASCOT ON SEX CHARGES

One thing you may notice about headlines is that they are short, especially in the tabloids where *impact* is required. In fact, if you examine some of the tabloid papers, the headline often takes up more space than the story itself.

They also have a kind of shorthand, a set of words often used to cover particular types of event or describe people.

For example,

When the United States bombed Libya in 1986 the *Sun* used the expression 'US RAMBO JETS' on its front page.

Words like *storm, fury, bust-up* are quick and simple but they may also exaggerate an emotion.

The *Sun* coined the expression 'Argies' for Argentinians. Nicknames are common in such papers and they may not always be very pleasant.

'Euro' is so commonly used now that we hardly notice that it is a shortened form of 'European'.

But don't take my word for it – look at the papers on a news stand or in a newsagent and compare the styles of the different papers.

Perhaps a better comparison would be to obtain copies of different newspapers for one day and examine them for content.

1 Make a note of the stories that appear in *all* the papers.
2 Compare the *language and style* used by different papers reporting the same story.
3 Compare the amount of space or prominence given to the stories: if two different types of paper carry the same story look also at the *number of words* devoted to the story and not just the space on the page.
4 Find stories that appear in one paper or type of paper and not in others.
5 Suggest reasons for these differences.

The electronic narcotic

Is television the same?

For example, is the content of TV programmes similar to that of the popular newspapers – mostly simple and undemanding?

The following TV guide was taken from the *Sun* (note the 'Wonderful World of *Sun* Telly' when they actually have nothing to do with the programmes at all). Can you see any similarities between this and the content of newspapers?

14   THE SUN, Monday, August 24, 1987   ☆ ☆ ☆ ☆

THE WONDERFUL WORLD OF Sun TELLY

| BBC1 | BBC2 | CHANNEL4 | CENTRAL | LONDON |

WISE UP ON THE SOAPS

Square stunner

ALBERT Square is stunned by the arrival of a pretty new face.

Heads turn when sexy Donna turns up looking for work in EASTENDERS (BBC1, Tues and Thurs, 7.30, repeat Sun, 2pm).

It was stated earlier that television companies claim to try to give a balanced view of the world.

Is this actually true?

It largely depends, it seems, on your viewpoint to start with. Both the extreme left and right of politics, for example, feel that the media are biased against them. But the very fact that a book like this can be published, asking all sorts of questions about the media and other issues, says something for our attitudes towards freedom of speech.

But as we saw right at the beginning of this chapter, what we know about the world may depend a lot on what other people *choose* to tell us – programme planners, editors and authors of books like this, for example.

Here are two examples – one real, one imaginary – of situations in which this kind of choice may be necessary.

1. *Real Lives*

In 1985 the BBC made a programme on Northern Ireland with the intention of showing the lives of two men who were involved on opposite sides in the politics of that province. It was due to go out on 7 August 1985.

One of the subjects of the programme was Gregory Campbell, a member of the right-wing, Protestant Democratic Unionist Party.

The other was Martin McGuinness, a member of the left-wing, republican Sinn Fein. He was also suspected of being a member of the chiefs of staff of the IRA.

The government objected to the programme being shown. Mrs Thatcher was against it on the grounds that it would give McGuinness a platform from which to speak. The Home Secretary at the time, Leon Brittain, wrote to the BBC expressing his opposition but also stating that he believed in the independence of the BBC to show whatever it chose as suitable viewing.

The programme was withdrawn amid accusations of government censorship; but after talks between the BBC and the government it was changed and eventually shown on 16 October.

So why did the government object?

(It is interesting that when the author was asking people about this incident, everybody remembered that it was a Sinn Fein man who was in the programme, and some even remembered his name, yet no one could remember who the Protestant man was.)

The programme had balance – the two men were on opposite sides of the political fence in Northern Ireland.

Does this mean that we are only willing to allow freedom of speech as long as what people say can't upset anyone?

Is it enough to have a balance *within* a programme or is it necessary to consider what types of programme should be screened at all?

2. What follows is totally imaginary but contains some of the problems faced by television companies and the government in deciding what should or should not be shown. Read the situation, then try the group exercise which follows and see what conclusion you come to.

A journalist working for an independent TV company receives an anonymous letter which tells him that the British government is involved in financing a terrorist organization in South America. He investigates further and finds out the following:

A member of the cabinet has recently visited country A where he spoke to a leader of the terrorist group which calls itself the ALS.

The ALS has been fighting the government of country B since a left-wing government took over some years ago. This government is heavily financed by the Soviet Union and backed Argentina with information and arms during the Falklands conflict.

The journalist has proof that arms sent to country A, a state friendly to Britain, have been given directly to the ALS.

The ALS has also been trained by members of the SAS, who have been involved on a regular basis since 1984.

There is a small community of British citizens living in country B, some of whom are likely to be involved in under-cover operations against the government.

Even those who are not – the majority – would find themselves in an awkward situation if such news was made public, even though the government of country B has long suspected British involvement with the ALS.

The British government has consistently pledged its opposition to all forms of terrorism, especially if sponsored by the state as in Libya.

Divide into groups and discuss the situation from the following points of view.

- The journalist who wants a programme on the affair to be screened. Try to imagine his motives – for both himself and Britain.
- The head of department at the TV company who has the power to give it the go-ahead. He or she may have mixed feelings. Would you be frightened in this position?
- The government. A tricky situation if you are confronted by such a programme (assume that it has been made). If you ban it you could be seen in a bad light.
    If you don't it could be a major scandal.
    Is there a way round the problem?
    How can you justify whatever you do?
- The viewer. Do you want to know about it?
    If it was never shown and never publicized you would be none the wiser, obviously, but would you be more likely to want to see it if it had been banned amid great publicity?
    Would you want to watch it if it received no more publicity than a mention in the *TV Times*?
    Would you miss your favourite programme to switch channels and watch it?

Speaking of viewers, how much say do they have in what's on?

▶ ▶ ▶ ▶ **FACT**

Here are some figures on the types of programmes shown. Do they surprise you?
How do they compare with your impressions from page 68?

Television programmes: by type, 1983–84 (United Kingdom)

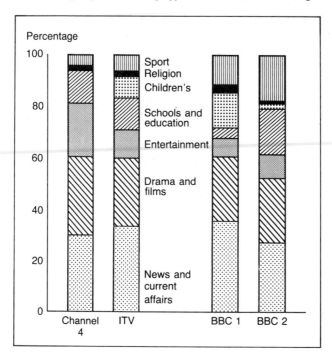

Source: *Social Trends* 16, 1986, London, HMSO.

▶ ▶ ▶ ▶ **SOMETHING TO DO**

Would *you* like to choose what is shown?

In groups (so as to avoid constant Eastenders) decide what you would put on in
the evenings between 7 and 11. Either choose particular programmes or the *type* of
programme you would like to see.

Now present your suggestions to the rest of the class.

● How much agreement was there?
● How much disagreement and why?
● Is there any similarity between what you would like and what is actually on?

You might now like to repeat the exercise, but this time do it from the point of
view of someone who is 25 years older than you.

Will this make a difference to your suggestions?

▶ ▶ ▶ ▶ TALKING POINT

You can't please all the people all of the time. Consider the following as topics for class discussion.

1 There should be a series of separate channels each showing a particular kind of programme all the time, e.g. a sports channel, a music channel, a current affairs channel, and so on.

2 There should be more channels with a mixture of programmes, as we have now. Each channel would have a general style (such as the difference between BBC 1 and BBC 2) and this would give us more variety.

3 Think also in terms of how it would be possible to control
   • The types of programmes shown so as to give a *genuine* mix.
   • The number of channels. (Would you like to have to choose between, say, 30 different channels?)

So who does decide?
And how accurately does television show the world to us?

▶ ▶ ▶ ▶ SOMETHING TO DO

Take for example the following stories:

1 An elderly woman is found murdered in her council flat.
2 A young girl writes to the Queen to ask if she can send someone to help her find her lost kitten.
3 The England cricket team wins the second Test match in Australia.
4 The government is criticized for its handling of a spy case.
5 Newly released police figures show a 5 per cent increase in crime in the last year.
6 A famous author dies.
7 The Prime Minister presents a local firm with an award for export achievement.
8 A group of Britons become trapped in a Middle Eastern country as a war breaks out.
9 House prices show a 20 per cent increase in the last year.
10 Sellafield nuclear waste re-processing plant is closed down temporarily after a leak.

Now imagine that you are the editor of the early evening news programme. What *order* would you put these items in?

The programme lasts 15 minutes. How much time would you give to each?

▶ ▶ ▶ ▶ THE POINT IS . . .

The *emphasis* we give to different types of news may influence the way we see the world around us.

For example, while crime has risen over the years it would seem that the *fear of crime* has increased even more.

▶ ▶ ▶ ▶ FACT

How many murders do you think are committed in Britain each year?

For the last five years or so the number has stayed about the same – around 500. Half of these are the result of family feuds.

Compare this to the 1,000 or so deaths among young people caused in some way by alcohol abuse.

Which one do you think is most likely to be reported?

Why?

▶ ▶ ▶ ▶ TALKING POINT

Do we live in a violent society?

Discuss your *feelings* about this then try to find information from books such as *Social Trends* as to the *real* level of different types of crime.

Do you think there is a connection between what is shown on television and reported in newspapers and people's behaviour?

In other words, can such things as violence and crime on TV influence the way people behave?

Some time ago a popular newspaper carried a sensational front page story on a vicious rape, talking indignantly about what a horrific crime it was. Fine.

In the same newspaper on the same day was a centre page spread on 'Women's top ten sexual fantasies'. The paper did not say how many women were interviewed or who the women were, but they did suggest very strongly that many of these were 'rape' fantasies, being 'taken' by some strong, dominant male (or even a group of them).

Was the paper *really* saying that women who are raped are usually willing partners and that it is as much their fault as anybody's?

▶ ▶ ▶ ▶ SOMETHING TO DO

Go back to your choice of types of programme (p. 76).

How many of them included violence of some kind?

Look through the programmes for a week and note down how often the programmes would usually include some form of violence. (You could do this in groups, taking different days so as to make it easier.)

▶ ▶ ▶ ▶ TALKING POINT

Is it possible that the way TV presents violence makes it unreal and therefore 'harmless'?

For example, The 'A' Team is a popular programme aimed mostly at a young audience that contains repeated scenes of violent clashes.

BUT . . .

We are being asked to believe that a crack, ex-Vietnam group of highly trained soldiers can repeatedly loose off about 500 rounds of machine-gun fire without actually hitting anyone.

Is this therefore purely harmless fantasy?

Discuss the idea that if violence *is* shown on television it ought to be as true to life as possible, showing horrific injuries, terrible pain and the suffering of the friends and family of the victims.

Would this make children less likely to want to copy what they see?

And has the fact that this book has chosen to highlight violence on TV made it seem much more of a problem than it really is? After all, there are lots of different types of programmes shown.

And we can always turn it off, can't we?

The information below shows how much time we spend watching 'the box'.

Television viewing: by age and sex (United Kingdom)

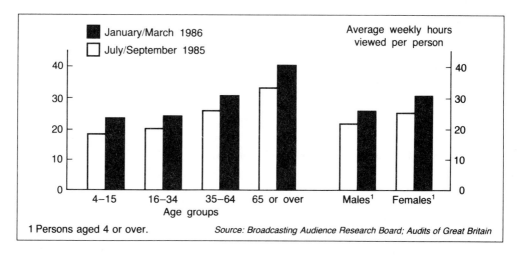

Source: *Social Trends* 17, 1987, London, HMSO.

It costs a lot of money to produce television programmes. In Britain the two organizations responsible for this are the BBC (British Broadcasting Corporation) and the IBA (Independent Broadcasting Authority).

They receive their money from two very different sources:

- The BBC is financed mostly by the television licence people are required to have by law if they want to operate a television set. In 1985 there were 18.7 million licences. Today they cost £58. This pays for BBC television and radio.
- The IBA gets its money mostly from advertising revenue. The actual amount it can charge for showing an advert will depend on the time of day and therefore the number of viewers it expects will be watching. (The system in the United States

is like this but they have many more channels in many more regions. But as an example of how income depends on audiences (or 'ratings') if a firm wanted to advertise during the live showing of the Super Bowl, a nationally broadcast football game, it would cost $1,200,000 per minute.)

The figures for some advertising rates on British TV are shown below and on p. 89, along with total spending on advertising.

You may notice that the time of day is more important than the actual programme being shown, but they would obviously put on their most popular programmes during peak times. They can then persuade the advertiser to part with large sums of money for the promise of an audience that is guaranteed to be, say, 15 million people.

▶ ▶ ▶ ▶ **TALKING POINT**

The IBA needs to produce popular programmes to survive; but what different does it make to the BBC if it produces a programme at peak time that only attracts 1 million people? After all, it already has their money from the licence fees.

Do you think the BBC would produce better programmes if it were allowed to advertise?

Fresh and natural at a new low price!

Advertising is big business as you can see from the table.

Total advertising expenditure by media

	1960		1975		1980		1983	
	£m	%	£m	%	£m	%	£m	%
National newspapers	64	19.8	162	16.8	426	16.7	584	16.3
Regional newspapers	77	23.8	283	29.3	640	25.0	817	22.8
Magazines and periodicals	40	12.4	79	8.2	192	7.5	224	6.3
Trade and technical	31	9.6	86	8.9	214	8.4	276	7.7
Other	17	5.2	69	7.2	212	8.3	335	9.4
Total press	229	70.9	679	70.2	1,684	65.9	2,236	62.5
TV	72	22.3	236	24.4	692	27.1	1,109	31.0
Poster and transport	16	5.0	35	3.6	107	4.2	137	3.8
Cinema	5	1.5	7	0.7	18	0.7	16	0.4
Radio	1	0.3	10	1.0	54	2.1	81	2.3
Total	323	100.0	967	100.0	2,555	100.0	3,579	100.0

Source: *AA Advertising Statistics Yearbook* 1984.

When firms spend this kind of money they obviously hope and expect that it will produce results – and it usually does.

▶ ▶ ▶ ▶ **SOMETHING TO DO**

Take twenty catch-phrases from TV adverts and ask people to name the product. You might find that they score well; some will even get them all right.

Not that this proves very much, but it does show that the advertisers can at least get us to remember the *name* of their products.

So *how* do they do it?

Advertising can take many forms, from the hugely expensive TV campaigns to the 'Under £10' column in your local paper.

We shall be dealing with the persuasive, expensive kind here rather than the simply informative.

The advertiser's intention is to make us *feel right* about a product. We must

- Know the name.
- Believe that it is what we want and need.
- Buy it.

It may sound strange, but we don't buy products. We buy *what the product will do for us*. They may

- Make our lives easier.
- Improve our image.
- Make us feel more secure.

In other words, make us feel *happier* with some aspect of our lives.

▶ ▶ ▶ ▶ **SOMETHING TO DO**

The table overleaf shows a list of methods advertisers use to plersuade us. Using the space on the right, write down the names of some products advertised in this way.

But before choosing a method, advertisers are limited in what they can do by an advertising code of practice. You may have seen the adverts put out by the Advertising Standards Authority. They ask people to let them know if they see an advertisement that is offensive or upsets them.

Basically adverts must be
- Legal
- Decent
- Honest
- Truthful

Have *you* ever seen an advert you think does not match up to these standards? If you look at some of the restrictions you might think that it is very difficult for advertisers to get their message across. For example:

- If you compare your product with someone else's you have to be able to *prove* what you say.

- You may not associate things such as tobacco or alcohol with success in, say, your love life or business.
- You cannot make incorrect claims – since there is no *cure* for the common cold you must describe it as 'for the relief of symptoms'.
- Adverts must conform to a standard of decency generally acceptable at the time.
- You may not frighten people for commercial gain, although public information films are allowed to worry people into being safety conscious.
- And so on . . .

But advertisers are very highly skilled in understanding 'what makes us tick' and they use very clever methods of presenting products so that we accept the image they are trying to get across.

The table shows a list of methods. Write in the name of a product you have seen advertised in this way.

Adverts are designed to appeal to our emotions and attitudes, for example:

Method	Product
Common sense – Factual information that demonstrates how good a product is, especially when compared to a competitor.	
Guilt – Are you doing the right things for your family? Are you the one to blame for things going wrong? Are you making others miserable?	
Envy – Fancy being the only person in your street without this product! Otherwise known as 'keeping up with the Joneses'.	
Greed – Go on! Splash out. There's nothing wrong with wanting to own as many things as you can (or even can't) afford.	
Self-image – Can you see yourself in this situation? Feeling more confident, more successful.	
Sense of humour – Laugh with the advert, feel happy and you will like the product. Advertisers know that people have 'favourite' ads.	

Continued

Method	Product
Fear – Close to guilt but they are not allowed to frighten us to death. The fear is normally of losing something – such as our health.	
Associations, endorsements – If our TV and sporting heroes and heroines recommend it, it must be good.	
Catch phrases and jingles – Have you ever started to hum a tune when you see a particular product in a shop? Children do – and advertise it at the same time.	

Of course, the advertisers mix them up so that using a film star to endorse a product may also be aimed at our self-image. *Sex* is often implied in adverts and may be mixed in with the methods mentioned above.

▶ ▶ ▶ ▶ **FOR EXAMPLE**

Minolta is a firm that makes, among other things, photocopiers. An advertising campaign they decided upon had two elements:

1 Their copiers have a zoom lens similar to that used in cameras (which they also make). To advertise this element of their machines they sponsored a series of athletics events, particularly sprinting.

   Thus zoom equals pace or speed. They are in fact, not related at all in this instance, but it does help the idea to stick in our minds.

2 They wanted to emphasize that their copiers were reliable. This is a very boring sort of subject, so they came up with the catch-phrase, 'Boringly Reliable'. So far so good. But how do you give that impact?

   The two words together could also describe Steve Davis, the snooker player. Many people think he is boring, but he is also a *winner*. Thus we have the image that what is boring can also be exceptionally good. And so Steve Davis was paid a lot of money to be associated with Minolta copiers on their adverts.

And this simply illustrates what is very important in advertising – *image*.

You may have found that when you were thinking about the different types of adverts to fit in with the methods on the previous page, there were certain *types* of products which came into each category.

It would be very difficult, for example, to advertise perfume in a factual way, or bring sex into washing powder adverts. Would you use scantily clad models to sell porridge? Would a film star agree to endorse those inserts that go into shoes to stop your feet smelling?

► ► ► ►   **SOMETHING TO DO**

In groups discuss and note down the style you would expect to find in adverts for the following items:

- Health food
- Domestic/kitchen appliances
- Perfume
- Drink
- Cars
- Airlines
- DIY tools
- A supermarket chain

Now discuss them as a class. Was there a general agreement on styles?
Now do the same again but this time discuss

- A style you think would *never* be used.
- A different style you think *could* work.

Then discuss your findings as a class.

Alongside image comes *language* as a way of creating that right impression.
Nothing in the advertising world can be seen as ordinary. This product must be different from all the others.
Nothing is simply brown, for example – it would have to be rich and golden as well.

► ► ► ►   **SOMETHING TO DO**

Can you turn the following words into advertiser's language?

- Cheap
- Expensive
- Fat
- Small
- Thin
- Heavy
- Flimsy
- Old
- Lazy
- Smell

And can you find adverts from magazines and newspapers and translate the language used there into English?

▶ ▶ ▶ ▶ TALKING POINT

- So how do advertisers see us, the general public?
- Are they insulting our intelligence by serving up these obviously false images?
- Or are we clever enough to see through it all and ignore it?

As was said before, someone must think it works – look at the amount of money they spend on it.

The advertisers tend to use *stereotypes* when putting their message across. They are usually restricted for time and space and so the snappy phrase or the 'familiar' situation are used to get us in the right frame of mind to accept what's coming next.

As we saw in Chapter 1 a stereotype is a general image which may hide the individual, even the truth.

▶ ▶ ▶ ▶ FACTS

A study carried out by Tony Manstead and Caroline McCulloch at Manchester University came up with some very interesting information about stereotyping in advertising.

They videotaped all the adverts in one week and eliminated repeats, leaving 170 different adverts to study.

They found that:

- 66 per cent of central characters, either in vision or voiced over, were male.
- 73 per cent of central figures shown at home were female.
- Men were mostly used to advance an argument for a product – women formed 62 per cent of figures who provided no argument at all, and only 19 per cent of those who advanced any kind of argument.
- Male central figures were less likely to appear in commercials for body, home and food products but they still dominated the adverts as authority figures by being used on voice overs – 94 per cent on body products, 83 per cent on home products and 89 per cent on food.
- In general women were portrayed as dependent on others (e.g. being seen as housewives), lacking in knowledge, product *users* rather than product authorities, and more likely to be seeking the approval of others through using certain products.
- Men, on the other hand, were shown as independent, knowledgeable, experts and in authority.
- While women make up 44 per cent of Britain's working population, they were shown in an independent role in only 13 per cent of adverts.

In other words, what the advertisers see as a 'normal' world may in fact be very far from the truth.

▶ ▶ ▶ ▶ TALKING POINT

- Does it really matter that certain sections of society are shown in a way which may not be typical?
- Does it do any harm? (Remember that children watch a lot of advertising and are more likely to be influenced by what they are seeing. They are more likely to accept it as 'real'.)

▶ ▶ ▶ ▶ EXAMPLE

There is an advert in which an over-worked technician is struggling to discover the secrets of how Canon can keep coming up with such advanced technology.

The technician, simply called 'Brains', is shown as a small, middle-aged man with untidy hair and half-moon glasses. (Stereotype?)

His helpers (who wear brown protective coats as opposed to 'Brains' who wears the white lab coat) keep wheeling in Canon machines with the phrase 'Another one for you to check out, Brains.'

One of the helpers is young, chirpy and black. The other is old.

If anyone objected to the advert on the grounds of racial discrimination – the black worker being the 'menial' – then most people would probably point out that it is at least a good thing that black people are portrayed as being in work and obviously working hard. And they might well be right. It is also true that black people as well as old, white people do menial jobs.

BUT . . .

Do you think the advertising company who made the commercial would have thought of making 'Brains' the young black man?

Try to imagine the advert with the black youngster in charge (it does happen in other adverts that young people are in charge) and with the older, white men as his assistants.

Or even try to imagine it with women in the same situation.

Do you think it would 'ring true'? Why?

▶ ▶ ▶ ▶ SOMETHING TO DO

Look at various adverts and change the central characters around. In some cases the results would obviously be ridiculous, but in others it might just be possible to see the man doing the cooking, the woman test driving the car, and so on . . .

AND . . .

It might also be possible to do it in such a way that it was not glaringly obvious that it was *unusual*.

▶ ▶ ▶ ▶ THE POINT IS . . .

Very few people would consider this Canon advert to be unusual or offensive in any way. We tend to accept it as just another advert.

▶ ▶ ▶ ▶ **SOMETHING TO DO**

In groups, plan an advertising campaign.
You can work on either

A – A new car which will be launched soon
or
B – A new range of kitchen equipment
(or both if you have the time)

In both cases you are allocated an initial budget of £250,000 for buying space in magazines or newspapers and air-time on television.
The choice of how and when the adverts go out is yours, but bear in mind

● The expected market (i.e. social class and income range of buyers).
● The image of the product and product user.
● The style of the campaign in relation to this market.

Details of the products are as follows:

A *The car*

Name – Blizzard. Manufacturer – Autotechnic (Germany)
Engine size – 1600 cc
Fuel consumption (independent test figures)
● Urban   33.5 mpg
● Constant 56 mph   42.7 mpg
● Constant 70 mph   31.4 mpg
Performance – 0–60 mph in 10.3 seconds, max speed 93 mph
Turbo version – 0–60 mph in 7.6 seconds, max speed 108 mph
No. of seats – 4/5
No. of doors – 3 or 5
Versions – saloon, hatchback, sport
   The sport version can also come in rally trim with a turbo-charged engine
Standard equipment – radio, laminated screen, rear seat belts, rear wash/wipe, central door locking, dual circuit brakes, cloth trim.
Price – standard GL   £7,289 + plates and delivery
       – rally sport   £8,879 +   "   "   "
       – turbo   £10,989 +   "   "   "

B *The kitchen equipment*

Manufacturer – Homewise UK Ltd
Range – Food processors, Microwave ovens, toasters.

Food processors: Basic model has 3 litre capacity bowl, two cutters (one for slicing, one for chopping) and single speed motor. Safety cut-out. Price: £34.99.

Microwaves: Basic version has 4 set power controls – full, roast, simmer and defrost. 45 minute dial timer. Power consumption – 1.1 kW.
Power output – 0.55 kW. Size – 500 mm × 300 mm × 290 mm. Price £159.00.
De-luxe version has variable power control, digital timer from 1 second to 1 hour, time delay. Power consumption – 1.3 kW. Output – 0.65 kW.
Size – 600 mm × 310 mm × 300 mm. Price £279.99.

Toasters – Basic; two slice, humidity sensor, automatic pop-up.
　Price – £14.99.
　De-luxe – three slice automatic humidity and size sensor, auto pop-up.
　Price – £27.99.

These details are only for guidance – you can use as many as you choose, but select the ones you need to put your message across.

Think in terms of *image* and *style*.

You will need to decide on

- The situations you are going to place any characters in.
- The method of getting the message across.

Produce

- A full page newspaper or magazine advert with impact and style.
- A 15–30 second TV advert with a rough story-board and script.

Prepare an explanation of where and when you will place the ads:

- Which paper and why?
- During which TV programmes and why?
- How you will spread the cost between TV and newspapers.

- Try to think up a slogan or catch-phrase to be used in both.
- Try to be different.

Then give an oral presentation to the rest of the class, explaining your reasons for your choice of style. If you can, ask someone not involved with the class to act as a director of the firm for whom you are producing the advert. He or she can then decide on which of the adverts they would use.

Remember: You must keep within the initial budget while achieving maximum *effective* coverage. Use the costs below.

Cost of advertising in national press

Name of newspaper	Cost of newspaper	Circulation	Cost of full page advertisement	Cost of half page advertisement
Daily Express	18p	1,988,339	£15,300	£7,800
Daily Mail	20p	1,837,521	£13,100	£6,930
Daily Mirror	16p	3,505,372	£23,130	£11,560
Daily Star	17p	1,501,945	£8,800	£4,600
Daily Telegraph	20p	1,252,847	£20,670	£10,600
Financial Times	35p	164,163	£15,904	£7,952
Guardian	23p	466,370	£13,200	£6,600
Sun	15p	4,150,191	£21,896	£10,948
Times	20p	381,075	£10,304	£5,152

Source: *Brad,* January 1985.

Cost of advertising on television

Peak viewing times: Monday to Sunday, 5.25 pm–10.25 pm
   30 seconds – £12,500
   60 seconds – £25,000

Off-peak viewing times: all other hours
   30 seconds – £6,400
   60 seconds – £12,800

7

Staying alive

By the end of this chapter the student should be able to:

1 Demonstrate an awareness of what constitutes a healthy diet.
2 Assess the benefits or dangers of a range of legal and illegal drugs.
3 Recognise the role of the food, brewing and tobacco industries in preserving or damaging our health.
4 Evaluate the extent to which our health is the responsibility of other people.
5 State the benefits, to the individual and society as a whole, of a healthy life-style.

Health is one of those things we often take for granted – until we fall ill. If we catch a cold we may simply endure the symptoms or buy a 'remedy' from a chemist, or, if it is something more serious, may have to enlist the help of a doctor or hospital. Organizations such as the Health Education Council exist to advise us on how not to fall ill while large companies in the tobacco industry exist to make money regardless of the possible damage to our health. In this chapter we examine some of the attitudes and ideas that are brought to bear on the issue, but first a few . . .

▶ ▶ ▶ ▶ **FACTS**

According to the statistics we live in a comparatively healthy society. *Infant mortality* is low, *average life expectancy* is high and awareness of health issues is good – many smokers, for example, admit that smoking is a dangerous habit. We have even managed to get rid of, or find a cure for, many of the infectious or contagious diseases which a hundred years ago killed people by the thousand. A great deal of time, effort and money is being spent on preventative medicine resulting in better public awareness of, for example, the need for a balanced diet or the dangers of drinking heavily.

Dying for a fag?

▶ ▶ ▶ ▶ **SOMETHING TO DO**

Look at the following table:

Adult smoking by sex and occupational group: percentage smoking cigarettes

	Professional	Employers and managers	Intermediate junior non-manual	Skilled manual and own account non-professional	Semi-skilled manual and personal service	Unskilled manual	All persons
Males							
1972	33	44	45	57	57	64	52
1976	25	38	40	51	53	58	46
1980	21	35	35	48	49	57	42
1982	20	29	30	42	47	49	38
1984	17	29	30	40	45	49	36
Females							
1972	33	38	38	47	42	42	42
1976	28	35	36	42	41	38	38
1980	21	33	34	43	39	41	37
1982	21	29	30	39	36	41	33
1984	15	29	28	37	37	36	32

Source: *Social Trends*, 1986, HMSO, London.

Now answer the following questions:

1 What has been the *general trend* in smoking habits since 1972?
2 Which group of people have always smoked most?
3 *Using only the figures in the table,* which of the following statements can be said to be true?

   (a) Men tend to smoke more than women.
   (b) Because of health worries, many people are giving up smoking.
   (c) People in higher paid jobs tend to smoke the least.
   (d) Smoking can seriously damage your health.
   (e) Smoking is less common than it used to be.

4 Draw a line graph of smoking trends from 1972 to 1984 using the 'all persons' figures for both men and women. (These figures can be taken as a general average.)
5 Find out how many members of the class smoke. Is this more or less than the averages shown in the table?

▶ ▶ ▶ ▶ **SOMETHING TO DO**

Answer the following questions by putting a tick under the appropriate heading.

	Agree	Don't know	Disagree
1 Smoking is bad because			
(a) It is expensive.	.....	....	....
(b) It is dangerous to your health.	.....	....	....
(c) It is dangerous to other people's health.	.....	....	....
(d) Non-smokers' taxes have to pay for health care for smokers.	.....	....	....
(e) It is a form of drug addiction.	.....	....	....
2 Smoking is good because			
(a) The industry employs thousands of people.	.....	....	....
(b) Tobacco tax revenue pays for much more than just health care for smokers.	.....	....	....
(c) It calms people down.	.....	....	....
3 Smoking should be banned in public places.	.....	....	....
4 Pregnant women should be prosecuted if they smoke.	.....	....	....
5 People should be allowed to choose for themselves if they want to damage their health by smoking.	.....	....	....
6 Smokers should be regarded as drug addicts and treated medically rather than being made to feel guilty.	.....	....	....
7 No tobacco company should be allowed to sponsor a sports event.	.....	....	....
8 The government health warning on cigarette packets should be more strongly worded.	.....	....	....

Now collect the results in and present them in a table showing how many people agree with each question. (You may find it interesting to divide the results between smokers and non-smokers.)

Are there any questions which *everyone* agreed with?

Why do you think this is?

You may now wish to extend the survey to the rest of the college/school. Include any other questions which you think it might have been useful to ask.

▶ ▶ ▶ ▶ **TALKING POINT**

What makes people smoke when they mostly agree it can be bad for them?

Can you suggest some of the reasons smokers would give for carrying on smoking? Or better still, ask them. Perhaps you could design a set of questions to put to smokers to find out

● Why they smoke.
● How they started.

- What they like about it.
- Whether the health hazards worry them.
- Whether they would like to give up.

▶ ▶ ▶ ▶ THE POINT IS . . .

Smoking is a much more complex issue than simply one of health. Because of what has happened in the past when people even thought that smoking could be *good* for you, it became a widespread social habit. The government now relies heavily on money raised in tobacco taxes but medical knowledge shows it would be better if nobody smoked.

▶ ▶ ▶ ▶ SOMETHING TO DO

In groups, discuss the viewpoints of the various people or organizations shown in the table – for example, how a non-smoking taxpayer may benefit indirectly from the massive tax revenues raised on tobacco – and present your findings to the rest of the class. Whether you think smoking is good or bad, you may at least see why it can be such a complicated issue.

	Benefits of smoking	Objections to smoking
Smokers	. . . .	. . . .
Taxpayers	. . . .	. . . .
Sports Council	. . . .	. . . .
Treasury (government)	. . . .	. . . .
National Health Service	. . . .	. . . .
Health Education Council	. . . .	. . . .
Tobacco companies	. . . .	. . . .

Warning: SMOKING CAN CAUSE
HEART DISEASE
Health Departments' Chief Medical Officers

Everybody likes a drink but nobody likes a drunk

Read the following statements:

- 'If alcohol had been invented yesterday, it would be banned today as a dangerous drug.'
- Many more young people die today from the effects of drink than from heroin addiction.
- 'I like a drink after work. It helps me to relax.'
- Drinking can seriously damage your health.
- Drink is a social habit. By relaxing people and helping them to forget their inhibitions it makes for a much more pleasant atmosphere.
- 'My doctor told me I'm in danger of becoming an alcoholic, but I know I can control it. I just enjoy a drink, that's all.'
- 'What I object to are these drink/driving laws. I reckon I'm a better driver when I've had a few.'
- 'Drink is like most other things in life – take it in moderation and it won't do you any harm.'

▶ ▶ ▶ ▶ **TALKING POINT**

In groups, try to imagine the viewpoint from which each statement was made and explain it to the rest of the class. It doesn't matter if you don't agree with the statement – simply try to work out what kind of person would say it and why.

Is there any consistent source of information, such as doctors, brewers or drinkers, that appears to come down on one side rather than another?

▶ ▶ ▶ ▶ **FACT**

Any book that deals with the question of drug dependency will include alcohol alongside drugs such as heroin, cannabis and cocaine, yet if we were to read a newspaper headline which stated *'THE DRUG MENACE AND BRITAIN'S YOUTH'*, few of us would think of drinking as being part of the problem – and it is unlikely that it would be part of the article anyway. If you turn to the definition of drugs on page 102 you will see that alcohol fits in very well – we take it at first for pleasure or benefit, it alters our perception and mental state and it is possible to become dependent on it. In fact in 1984 Alcoholics Anonymous had about 35,000 clients, although it is likely that there are ten times as many alcoholics as this – at least.

▶ ▶ ▶ ▶ **TALKING POINT**

So – what is an alcoholic?

How would *you* define an alcoholic? By how much they drink? Or how often? By how often they get drunk?

Would a doctor's view of an alcoholic be different from that of a brewery director?

► ► ► ► **FACT**

Some people would argue that smoking is mostly an individual choice which, by and large, only damages the smoker. Could the same be said of drinking? Look at some of the consequences.

- Alcohol 'preserves' living tissue. What are the results of this for the human body?
- Alcohol stops the brain working normally. Walking, standing and driving will suffer but we may not even realise it.
- Alcohol is a depressant drug – that is, it slows you down – but its first effect is to stimulate and at least give the feeling of well-being. When can this be useful socially?
- About three-quarters of assaults are related to drink, as are half of the murders committed in this country.
- Going out for a drink is the single most common leisure activity people participate in outside the home.
- The legally acceptable level of blood alcohol for drivers of cars is *twenty* times higher than that allowed for private aircraft pilots. Is flying that much more dangerous than driving, or are we too lenient on car drivers?

► ► ► ► **SOMETHING TO DO**

When do you think a drinker reaches the stage of being dependent on alcohol?

In groups, examine the following descriptions and decide which you think is a profile of an alcoholic.

A. Female. Aged 26. Local government officer. Slim, lively, occasionally nervy. A very light eater. Enjoys going out with her friends, drinks only as much as them and never gets drunk but does go out every night. Always arrives in the pub before her friends. Has had a lot of time off work this year for such things as back strains, a cut hand and stomach upsets. Her flatmate recently found three empty spirit bottles in the waste bin and also learned she had been lying about the time she had taken off work.

B. Male. 52. Building worker. Overweight and very red-faced. Occasionally drinks at lunchtime, but always goes to the pub in the evenings where he will drink between six and eight pints of beer. Never drinks wine or spirits. Eats well and usually spends Saturday and Sunday afternoons asleep after a lunchtime session.

C. Male. 38. Office worker. Drinks every lunchtime but does not always go out at night, although will have a few glasses of beer while watching television. Averages 4 or 5 pints of beer a day, spread over the whole day. Rarely seen to be drunk. Eats only one good meal a day. Prefers to drink late in the evening just before going to bed. Only drinks beer in the pub but will drink wine with a meal and spirits at Christmas.

D. Male. 33. Teacher. Has drunk socially since he was 16. Does not smoke, keeps fit with a variety of sports and is very careful about his vegetarian diet. Drinks heavily but always in a social, friendly way. Will get drunk at social gatherings such as friends' birthday celebrations but has a higher tolerance of drink than most people and can therefore seem quite sober and sensible when all around him are drunk.

Do you think your assessment would be different if you were a doctor? Or a friend and 'drinking partner' or these people? Or a close relative?

Under-age drinking

In general terms the law states that you are not allowed to go into a public house and buy intoxicating liquor for yourself or anyone else if you are under 18 years old. (What are the exceptions to this?)

▶ ▶ ▶ ▶ SOMETHING TO DO

In fact, many people under 18 do drink in pubs. Your task now is to examine this situation from a variety of viewpoints. The class should be divided into five groups and each should imagine the situation from the point of view of the person or people listed. Write down as many arguments as you can think of which support the view of *the person or persons you are supposed to be*. (Those listed under the following groups are only *suggestions* as to what you might discuss. How many more can you think of?)

- *A 17-year-old* – Why do you want to go into the pub? What is your objection to the law?
- *The police* – Will you always prosecute every case you are aware of, or even suspect?

- *A publican* – What does the law say about *your* role in under-age drinking? How could you benefit or suffer from it?
- *The brewery* – Whose responsibility is it to uphold the law? Do you mind as long as the money is coming in?
- *The government* – Is the age limit a reasonable one, bearing in mind the other things that people are allowed to do before they are 18? What would voters think if you lowered the age?

By the way, *all* the people described on page 95 would be considered by a medical person to have a drink problem, but in varying degrees.

A shows the classic symptoms of acute alcoholism – constant drinking but with few outward signs and with a series of deceptions for friends and employers. It is a fact that many people who live with alcoholics are unaware of the fact for a long time.

B is certainly a heavy drinker – but is he *dependent* on drink, or is it simply a habit?

C may not appear to be a heavy drinker but there are signs of dependence. Is the lunchtime drinking for relief of stress and is the evening drinking an attempt to relax and help him sleep?

D is obviously aware of his drink problem judging by the way he looks after his health in other ways – or is he? Is he fooling himself that because he is careful about health in other ways he can control his drinking?

So what are our attitudes to drink?

▶ ▶ ▶ ▶ **SOMETHING TO DO**

Try the following, each of which could be a class, group or individual project.

1 Divide into groups and obtain information from a variety of sources about drink, e.g. Brewers' Society, government revenue figures, the Teachers' Advisory Council on Alcohol and Drug Education, the Health Education Council. Either write to interested organizations or obtain the relevant information from the library.
2 Examine

- Drinks advertising.
- Anti-drink lobbies and pressure groups.
  What lies behind their approach to drinking?

3 Report your findings to the rest of the class.
4 Again in groups and using this information, present an argument for
   - Relaxing the current licensing laws.
   - Restricting further the sale of alcoholic drinks.
   - An educational campaign similar to that carried out by the anti-smoking lobby.
   - The social benefits of drinking (i.e. what would society be like without alcohol, seen from the point of view of someone who likes to drink?).

You are what you eat

'You are what you eat' is a relatively common expression nowadays and is meant to emphasize the idea that our bodies are simply collections of substances we get from our food. It has another meaning as well and that is that if you eat 'junk' or 'bad' food it will somehow damage you. Some of the things currently thought to be bad for us include cholesterol, salt, sugar and a whole range of additives, many of which have an 'E' number. A greater awareness of the potential damage we may suffer from what we eat, plus pressures from people who are also *concerned* about it, has led to a series of food labelling regulations designed to let us know what it is we are eating.

Does this therefore mean that we are likely to choose a healthier diet?

Is it enough to know that E122 is being used in this packet of whatever, or should we be told exactly what the likely effects will be?

'Eat more fibre' is considered to be good advice, but why?

And have manufacturers of packaged foods jumped on the bandwagon by proclaiming that, for example, a packet of crisps contains no artificial colouring, preservatives or flavourings? Are the crisps themselves potentially dangerous?

In short, should some food packets carry a government health warning?

What is this, for example?

● Starch, salt, colours E102, E110, E127, flavourings

Good nutrition is all about *balance*. No food can in itself be dangerous. But a diet that consisted entirely of hamburger, chips and beans would not be very beneficial and could actually be harmful.

What do *you* eat?

► ► ► ► **SOMETHING TO DO**

In the following chart, write in the kind of food you would typically eat in a week –
this will probably vary, of course, but in general it will give a picture of your dietary
pattern.

	Sunday	Monday	Tuesday	Wednesday	Thursday	Friday	Saturday
Breakfast							
Midday meal							
Evening meal							
Snacks, sweets, etc.							
Drinks							

Now, in groups, pick out the most common foods you all eat as main meals, along
with sweets and drinks.

THEN . . .

Try to find out what harmful or doubtful substances are added to them, or if there
are any problems with them – for example, caffeine in tea and coffee, preservatives
in crisps or the animal fats chips are cooked in. This sort of information will
normally be available on the packets or in books on nutrition.

Compare this to the diet of the working-class family in York in 1899.

From a survey carried out in York in 1899, Seebohm Rowntree (yes, the same
family as the sweets manufacturer) discovered the following information about a
typical diet of a family in poverty.

Meal	Saturday	Sunday	Monday	Tuesday	Wednesday	Thursday	Friday
Breakfast	Bread butter boiled egg coffee	Bread butter Coffee	Bread butter coffee	Bread butter tea	Bread butter coffee	Bread butter coffee	Bread butter tea
Lunch/ dinner	Meat pie Potatoes Tea	Beef Potatoes Pudding Tea	Meat Potatoes Bread Tea	Hash Bread Tea	Liver Potatoes Onions Tea	Bread Dripping Tea	Bread Butter Toast Tea
Tea	Bread Butter Tea	Bread Butter Tea	Bread Butter Tea	Bread Butter Tea	Bread Butter Dripping Tea	Bread Dripping Tea	Bread Butter Tea
Supper	Roast potatoes Tea	Meat Bread Tea					

From your examination of your own diet, is there anything in here which you would now think of as being harmful?

And is there anything which you think could be seriously lacking?

▶ ▶ ▶ ▶ **FACT**

The following information was taken from the packaging of various foodstuffs. Can you guess what the foods are?

1 Sugar solution, citrus fruits (orange, lemon, mandarins), water, fructose, passion fruit juice, apricots, gelling agent – amidated pectin, malic acid, preservative – potassium sorbate, antioxidant – ascorbic acid.

2 Sugar, modified starch, hydrogenated vegetable oil, emulsifiers E477, E322, gelling agents E399, E450a, caseinate, lactose, whey powder, flavourings, salt, caramel, colours E102, E122, E160a, antioxidant E320.

3 Potatoes, edible vegetable oils (with hydrogenated vegetable oil), antioxidants E320, E321, seasoning, flavourings, salt, flavour enhancer (monosodium gluta-mate), citric acid.

4 Wholemeal flour, vegetable fat, yeast extract, salt, cheese, wheat starch, pepper.

5 (a) Wheatflour, shortening (animal fat, vegetable oil), water, salt.
   (b) Water, beef, kidney, modified starch, soya flour, salt, hydrolyzed vegetable protein, spices, colour (caramel), flavour enhancer 621.

6 Carbonated water, sugar, colour (caramel), phosphoric acid, flavourings, caffeine.

7 Hydrolyzed protein, wheatflour, yeast extract, salt, colour (caramel), beef stock, flavour enhancers E621, E635, beef fat, beef extract, sugar, vegetable oil, lactic acid, pepper, onion powder.

8 Milk chocolate, sugar, glucose syrup, vegetable fat, cooked rice with added wheatgerm, wheat flour, sweetened condensed skimmed milk, butterfat, salt, flavourings, emulsifier (lecithin), yeast, raising agent (sodium bicarbonate), calcium sulphate.

9 Wheatflour, butter, sugar, liquid whole eggs, coconut, cocoa, cocoa butter, salt, vanilla.

10 Dried potato, dried skimmed milk, salt, vegetable oil and partial glycerol esters (both contain permitted antioxidants), emulsifying salt, sodium sulphate, pepper.

Remember that the ingredients are arranged in order of quantity, i.e. the item that comes first is the largest single ingredient.

● Oh, by the way, the foodstuff on page 98 was Birds' custard.

Much of what we eat nowadays is 'convenience' food and many people are worried that our health may suffer from eating stodge and additives from tins and packets. The word 'malnutrition' is something most people would associate with starvation in other, poorer countries, but a person who is *over*weight could be suffering from malnutrition.

Malnutrition occurs when there is an imbalance in the diet, as there would be if someone ate more sweets, crisps and fizzy drinks, which are marketed mostly for the young, than anything else. The assumption that we are a well fed nation has had its critics recently, especially now that many family diets are based heavily on packaged foods, so that many children, if a well balanced and nutritious diet is not available at school, eat badly. Now that school meals are so expensive such children may make do with perhaps a bag of chips at lunchtime, which may be filling but that's about all they are.

Another problem is that even the things which we have long thought of as being good for us are considered by some to have harmful effects. For instance, it is now known that red meat such as beef, along with eggs and milk, contain cholesterol, which is known to contribute to heart and circulatory problems by 'furring' arteries.

So-called 'natural' foods such as fruit and vegetables may contain or be covered in various anti-fungal chemical sprays. Even meat may contain high levels of antibiotics, which are added to the animals' feed to keep them 'healthy'.

So how can we eat well and remain healthy?

▶ ▶ ▶ ▶ **SOMETHING TO DO**

Find out what constitutes a healthy diet. (This information will normally be available from the library, from *Which?* magazine, home economics books or newspaper and women's magazine articles.)

In general we need protein, carbohydrates and fat along with vitamins and some small amounts of minerals. But in what proportions?

And are all proteins or fats the same?

You will get carbohydrates from bread, but is one type of bread better for you than another?

If you doubt the importance of diet, you need only look at the statistics on how common or rare various illnesses are in different countries to see that what people eat and the way they eat it can lead to health problems.

For example, the incidence of bowel cancer in Japan is very low compared to many other industrial countries, and this is thought to be related to the way the Japanese cook their food.

▶ ▶ ▶ ▶ **TALKING POINT**

Can the British style of eating do us harm? How can we avoid problems?

As a guide, think back to the things you eat and any information you have found out about various foods.

- Answers to the ingredients on page 100.
  1. *Reduced sugar* marmalade. 2. Angel Delight. 3. Cheese and onion crisps. 4. Twiglets. 5. Steak and kidney pie (a = crust, b = filling). 6. Coca-Cola. 7. Oxo cubes. 8. Lion bars. 9. Danish biscuits. 10. Instant mashed potato.

Drugs

'Sex and drugs and rock and roll are all my brain and body need' – Ian Dury

Just the mention of the word 'drugs' is often enough to conjure up images of usually young people behaving in a variety of anti-social ways; either creating disturbances in public or tucked away in quiet places damaging their minds and bodies with 'certain substances'. There are, however, many sorts of drugs. The pharmaceutical companies that manufacture them are among the largest companies in the world.

Which of the following do you regard as being a drug?

● Tea	● Beer	● Marijuana	● Cocaine
● Valium	● Aspirin	● Mescaline	● Clothes
● LSD	● Coffee	● Barbiturates	● Amphetamines
● Heroin	● Cigarettes	● Television	

Why?

Drugs have been defined by one writer as any chemical substance that alters mood, perceptions or consciousness and is *misused* to the apparent detriment of society.

Most other definitions would add the idea of *dependence* on the substance.

▶ ▶ ▶ ▶ **TALKING POINT**

Would it be fair to say that it is only the word 'chemical' that disqualifies television from being defined as a drug? Clothes, on the other hand, can be seen as things on which we are dependent, especially in the winter, and we also wear them for benefit or pleasure. Torturers also know that the removal of clothes from victims can give rise to symptoms of distress such as occur when barbiturates or alcohol are withdrawn. And could so-called junk food come into this category?

▶ ▶ ▶ ▶ **SOMETHING TO DO**

Below is a list of drugs it is currently illegal to use without medical prescription or supervision. Find out what their *effects* are on both the mind and body and note them down in the space provided, examining both effects of *use* and *withdrawal*.

This information will be available from various sources in libraries or local help organizations.

Drug	Effects of use	of withdrawal
Opium	. . . .	. . . .
Morphine	. . . .	. . . .
Heroin	. . . .	. . . .
Cocaine	. . . .	. . . .
Marijuana	. . . .	. . . .
Hashish	. . . .	. . . .
Amphetamines	. . . .	. . . .
Barbiturates	. . . .	. . . .
LSD	. . . .	. . . .
Caffeine	. . . .	. . . .
Nicotine	. . . .	. . . .
Alcohol	. . . .	. . . .

▶ ▶ ▶ ▶ **FACTS**

In 1984, 395,600,000 prescriptions were dispensed at an average cost per prescription of £4.42.

The outflow of money from the United States to buy illegal drugs was once likened to the cost of fighting a small war.

But how might your attitude to drugs change if you knew that about 300 people a year die from *aspirin* poisoning?

The number of deaths as a result of cancer is very high – over 1 in 5 of people dying between the ages of 20 and 70 – but how many of those might have been the result of taking prescribed drugs such as the contraceptive pill? (The numbers *are* higher amongst women.)

▶ ▶ ▶ ▶ **SOMETHING TO DO**

Do a similar exercise to that for smoking (page 93), i.e. in groups note down the different viewpoints (favourable and unfavourable) for the following drugs as you might expect would be expressed by the groups or organizations mentioned.

	User	Manufacturer	Police	Government	Doctor
Marijuana	....	....	....	....	......
Tobacco	....	....	....	....	......
Morphine	....	....	....	....	......
Paracetamol	....	....	....	....	......
Valium	....	....	....	....	......
Amphetamines	....	....	....	....	......
LSD	....	....	....	....	......
Alcohol	....	....	....	....	......

Try to think in terms of both the benefits and problems which apply in each case, e.g. morphine, LSD and amphetamines are all used medically.

Who might benefit or lose financially from the legal and illegal use of drugs?

What initial benefit does the user get?

And what long-term damage may result?

Is it possible to make out a case for legalizing cannabis, or should a similar argument be used for banning alcohol or tobacco?

▶ ▶ ▶ ▶ **TALKING POINT**

So whose responsibility is our health? On the surface it would appear that it is a person's own fault if he or she smokes, drinks too much and over-eats, or takes drugs. But knowledge of health matters has greatly increased in recent years and medical research is continuing to raise many more questions about how we look after ourselves and the causes of health problems.

It is possible, for instance, to argue that the government could take a more prominent role in educating the public. After all, it is in their interests to have a healthy population – fewer days would be lost at work , there would be more revenue from higher earnings, and less money spent on the health service. But then, smoking and drinking produce very high levels of income from excise duties and VAT, and the longer people live, the more must be spent on pensions.

The Health Education Council were recently critical of the government for failing to show any interest in educating the public about the dangers of alcohol abuse.

Could this have been because the Conservative Party receive some very large donations from breweries, and drinks tax revenue is very high? Or simply because, in their considered opinion, drinking is a socially acceptable activity and abuses are over-emphasized?

Here are some facts and figures that may help you to decide.

- In 1985/86 the government spent about £38,000 million on social security, over £19,000 million on health and social services, a similar sum on defence and about £16,000 million on education. (This includes expenditure by local government.)
- In 1984 total receipts from such things as income tax, VAT and taxes on spending, rates and National Insurance, was £146,000 million.
- People's spending on tobacco in 1984 was £6,621 million.
- £14,416 million was spent on alcoholic drink (in other words, over £21,000 million on legal drugs, not to mention caffeine) while £28,448 million went on food and £13,000 million on clothes.
- A man born in 1901 could expect to live to the age of 48 (average life expectancy) while life expectancy for anyone born now is 70 for males and 76 for females.

Narcotic drugs – new addicts notified* by age and sex (United Kingdom)

	Under 20	20–24	25–29	30–34	35–49	50 or over	Not known	Total
Males								
1973	149	334	89	23	20	24	5	644
1976	61	315	251	55	35	20	8	745
1981	141	544	511	269	78	15	49	1,607
1982	197	676	593	323	118	16	53	1,976
1983	402	1,011	766	440	192	38	130	2,979
1984	584	1,334	958	570	257	22	115	3,840
Females								
1973	41	79	20	7	8	8	0	163
1976	40	100	55	15	10	12	7	239
1981	91	225	186	84	18	14	23	641
1982	113	271	233	113	41	12	34	817
1983	170	446	315	150	59	18	49	1,207
1984	214	618	405	205	63	19	51	1,575

* New addicts notified to the Home Office during the year.

Source: *Social Trends* 16, 1986, London, HMSO.

Selected causes of death: by sex and age, 1951 and 1984 (United Kingdom)

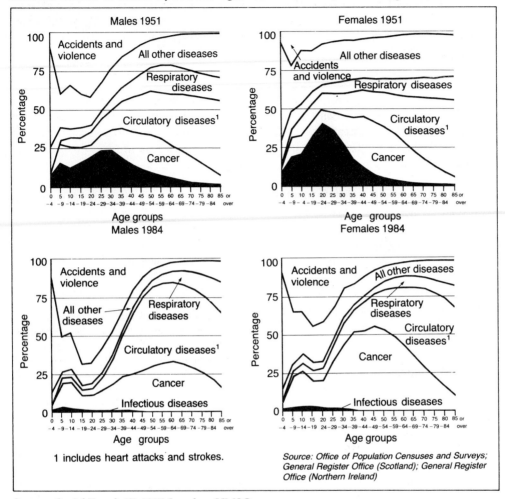

1 includes heart attacks and strokes.

Source: Office of Population Censuses and Surveys; General Register Office (Scotland); General Register Office (Northern Ireland)

Source: *Social Trends* 17, 1987, London, HMSO.

Alcohol misuse – admissions to mental illness hospitals and units: by sex and age, 1983 (United Kingdom)

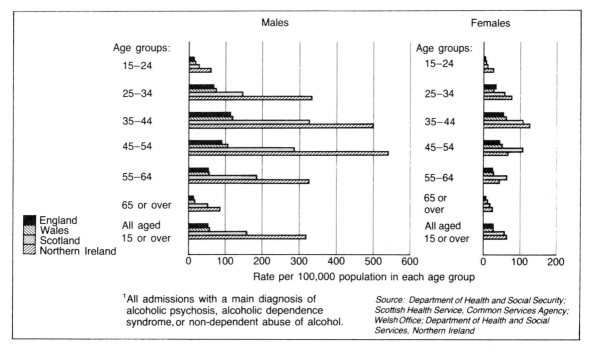

¹All admissions with a main diagnosis of alcoholic psychosis, alcoholic dependence syndrome, or non-dependent abuse of alcohol.

Source: Department of Health and Social Security; Scottish Health Service, Common Services Agency; Welsh Office; Department of Health and Social Services, Northern Ireland

Source: *Social Trends* 16, 1986, London, HMSO.

▶ ▶ ▶ ▶ **TALKING POINT**

Use these graphs, along with what you may have found out up to now, to discuss the following:

● 'If the government spent as much on general health education as it did on its "AIDS" campaign, we would all be a lot healthier and they would save money in the long run by not having to look after so many sick people.'

8

Have you got a minute?

By the end of this chapter the student should be able to:
1 Recognise the need for leisure time.
2 Assess the influences on our choice of leisure activity.
3 Assess the extent to which different leisure activities carry different status.
4 Examine his/her own use of leisure time.

You may have heard people talk about the leisure industry, even a 'leisure boom'. The amount of time we have to ourselves to do with as we please has been increasing gradually throughout this century and it will probably continue to do so.

But how much free time do we really have?

And what do we do with it?

▶ ▶ ▶ ▶ **SOMETHING TO DO**

Below is a chart showing time used in a typical week for different groups of people. It is divided into time spent in:

- *Work*, including travel to and from the workplace.
- *Essential activities*, which include personal care, shopping, domestic work, cooking and eating, and so on.
- *Sleep*.
- *Free time*.

Study the figures and answer the questions that follow.

Time use in a typical week: by economic status, Spring 1985

	Full-time employees		Part-time employees		Housewives
	Males	Females	Males	Females	
Weekly hours spent on:					
employment and travel	45.0	40.8	24.3	22.2	—
essential activities	33.1	45.1	48.8	61.3	76.6
sleep	56.4	57.5	56.6	57.0	59.2
free time	33.5	24.6	38.3	27.5	32.2
Free time/weekday	2.6	2.1	4.5	3.1	4.2
Free time/weekend day	10.2	7.2	7.8	5.9	5.6

Source: *Social Trends* 16, 1986, London, HMSO.

1 Why do you think housewives have less free time than full-time male employees?
2 Why do you think part-time employees spend so much more time in essential activities than full-time employees?
3 What, if anything, do the figures tell us about the division of work in the home (essential activities)?
4 The self-employed are not included in these figures. What differences would you expect to find if their time was analysed in this way?
5 How does this chart compare to *your* use of time in a week? Do you spend more or less time in any of the activities shown? Why?

Perhaps you could analyse your time by drawing up a chart showing the hours you spend in these activities. But instead of simply calling it 'free time' you could make a note of exactly what you do.

(If you are at school you can substitute school time for 'employment and travel'.)

For example, show the time you spend watching television, listening to the radio, playing a sport, reading and so on. You could then compare this with the information in the rest of this chapter.

But what is it that influences our choice of leisure activities?

▶ ▶ ▶ ▶ **SOMETHING TO DO**

Draw up a list of the things that affect our patterns of leisure. In small groups, discuss and note down:

1 The kinds of things virtually anyone can do with his/her free time.
2 The kinds of things usually done by only certain groups of people, such as young people, men or women.
3 The kinds of things done by only very small numbers of people.

Then try to work out why. In other words, if virtually everyone could spend a lot of time reading books – they are easily available from libraries and just about everyone in Britain can read – why don't they? What are the kinds of things that would *stop* us from getting involved in particular acitivies?

Make a note of your ideas on a chart similar to the one below, then discuss them as a class. (Some examples are included to get you started.)

Type of activity	Availability	Who does it	What would stop others
Watching TV	Open to virtually anyone	Most people	Dislike content of programmes
Playing soccer	Usually for certain groups only	Mostly young men	Age and fitness; prejudice against women's teams
Fox-hunting	Only for very small groups	Mostly wealthy/ 'aristocratic' people	Lack of money; disagree with it; not 'brought up' to it.

Below is a table showing a selection of leisure activities by sex and age. The figures are percentages of people in each age group taking part in the named activity in the four weeks before the survey (1983).

	Males					Females				
	16–19	*20–34*	*35–59*	*60+*	*All*	*16–19*	*20–34*	*35–59*	*60+*	*All*
Open air outing to										
country	1	2	3	3	3	2	3	3	3	3
parks	2	4	3	2	3	3	8	3	2	4
Entertainment, social and cultural activities										
Going to the cinema	17	13	5	1	7	25	13	5	2	8
Going to theatre/opera /ballet	2	4	4	3	4	5	5	7	4	5
Amateur music/drama	6	4	3	2	3	6	3	3	2	3
Attending leisure classes	1	1	2	1	1	1	2	3	2	2
Going out for a meal	39	47	42	31	41	44	46	44	29	40
Going out for a drink	68	82	65	41	64	72	67	49	18	46
*Home-based activities**										
Listening to records/ tapes	93	81	65	40	65	94	80	67	32	62
Gardening	20	39	58	59	50	13	36	49	37	39
House repairs/DIY	31	55	61	39	51	12	31	30	13	24
Reading books	44	49	51	51	50	62	62	62	59	61

* For details of television viewing, see Chapter 6, page 79.

Source: *Social Trends* 16, London, HMSO.

We can see from this chart that a person's age and sex will affect the type of leisure activity chosen.

But is there anything else?

If you study the table you can see some 'obvious' differences, such as young people being much more likely than older people to listen to records and tapes. Perhaps you would expect men to go out for a drink more than women.

But what about the *type* of activity?

For example, the number of people going to the theatre or ballet is very small across all age groups, as is attending leisure classes. Is there anything other than sex or age that will influence what we do?

How, for example, might our job (or lack of one) influence what we do with our spare time?

▶ ▶ ▶ ▶ **SOMETHING TO DO**

Below is a list of activities that may be affected by what we do for a living. In small groups, fill in the spaces in the chart (or something similar).

In the first space make a note of the type of job the person might do who takes part in the activity.

In the next write in what you think the reason for this is. Does it always come down to money? For example, does the way the activity is organized make a difference to who would participate?

The 'job' categories you should use for consistency are:
● Professional, employers and managers
● Intermediate, non-manual workers
● Skilled manual and self-employed manual
● Semi- and unskilled manual
● Unemployed/training scheme students
● Full-time students

Activity	Who takes part	Why them more than others?
Football	. . . .	. . . .
Golf	. . . .	. . . .
Athletics	. . . .	. . . .
Rugby	. . . .	. . . .
Cricket	. . . .	. . . .
Fishing	. . . .	. . . .
Sailing	. . . .	. . . .
Darts	. . . .	. . . .
Snooker	. . . .	. . . .
Horse riding	. . . .	. . . .
Swimming	. . . .	. . . .
Tennis	. . . .	. . . .

Perhaps you could add in some of your own if you think it would help.

Having thought about *who* does *what* and *when* it is now time to look at *why*.

What is the importance of leisure time? Nowadays we tend to take it for granted that we have time to ourselves to do with as we please, but how much choice do we really have?

For example, a lack of money may mean that we cannot take part in certain activities. Or it may be that an organization is not available to help bring people together.

In his book *Brave New World*, Aldous Huxley wrote of a future society divided into strict social categories. Those at the top had the best of everything and plenty of time to do as they pleased – as long as their leisure involved the use of equipment and goods. It was a society that depended on high levels of industrial production. Activities like going for a walk to enjoy the countryside were frowned upon because they did not need anyone to produce anything. Leisure of this kind did not keep people in jobs.

Go back to the list of your own leisure activities from page 109 and make a note of *why* you do them.

How many of them are for helping you relax?

If you take part in a sport, what do you get out of it?

How often are you *active* in what you do? In other words, which activities need some kind of effort on your part? (This could include reading or a hobby such as woodworking or painting. It doesn't have to be hard physical effort.)

How much of your leisure involves mental rather than physical effort?

▶ ▶ ▶ ▶ TALKING POINT

Discuss your answers to these questions as a class and then consider the following points:

- For most of our leisure we depend on other people – sports goods manufacturers, TV programme producers, musicians, breweries, authors, and 'experts' in our chosen activity, etc.
- Most of our leisure is a contrast to what we normally do for a living or during the day – people who work in offices spend more time taking part in sport than people who do heavy physical work; manual workers are more likely to want to relax in the pub or watch television.
- But does this also mean that manual workers are more likely to read books than, say, a teacher or manager? Why?
- In short, is it true that, like so many other things in life, what we can get out of our leisure time depends on our 'social class'?
- So how might we get more out of our leisure time?

▶ ▶ ▶ ▶ SOMETHING TO DO

Imagine that you are members of a council sub-committee in the Recreation Section and have been asked to consider the problem of leisure provision within your area.

The local authority has made it known that money is available for a complete review of leisure facilities and has asked for suggestions on how to allocate this money.

First read the following documents and tables.

Document A:
Extract from the minutes of local council meeting held on 19 November.

Mrs Mary Tolworth, leader of the council, presented a discussion document to the meeting which outlined the proposed increases in expenditure for the coming year. She drew particular attention to the section on 'Leisure, Recreation and Community Facilities' which she pointed out had been neglected in recent times; and she urged acceptance of the £5 million increase in provision over the next 3 years on the following grounds:

1. It should be the duty of the council to take a lead in looking after *all* the interests of local residents – not just roads and rates but the enjoyable things in life as well.
2. This expenditure would merely restore to a reasonable level the provision of facilities which had been allowed to run down in the past.
3. It could have positive effects in providing local employment and also generating income for local businesses provided the money were well spent.
4. It would go some of the way to improving the quality of people's lives. It could, for example, provide worthwhile activities for the young, either as participants or in helping to set up various schemes. It may even have hidden benefits such as reducing the levels of vandalism and nuisances committed by bored youngsters.

Finally she added that its success depended on the support of the council and the quality of the provision, and to this end she intended to set up a working party to produce ideas for the council's approval.

Document B:
Report of the council meeting which appeared the following day in the local evening newspaper.

A council meeting broke up amid storms of protest from angry opposition councillors last night. They were responding to Mrs Tolworth's presentation of a new £5 million package of spending on leisure facilities in the borough.

The council leader's view was that it would be a worthwhile project for the benefit of all, but the opposition's doubts centred on what they regard as wastefulness. Ted Walmsley, local shopkeeper and councillor for Downton ward, called it 'a waste of ratepayers' money when what was needed was work and trade for the many, not idle pleasure for the few'.

Some councillors did receive it with a reserved enthusiasm, saying that it was about time something was done for the whole community but worrying as well that it might turn into an expensive and under-used provision.

Document C:
Extracts from letters to the newspaper from local residents.

- 'I think it's a great idea. It's about time more was done for the youngsters of this town. At the moment there's only an overcrowded sports hall and an ancient swimming pool.' (Jane Wilson, 16)

- 'I only hope Mrs Tolworth is really thinking of everyone with this scheme. It's about time we had more community centres for the young and the old. As a mum with pre-school children I'd welcome the idea of getting out of the house a bit more.' (Pauline Smith, 26)

- '. . . a scandalous waste of ratepayers' money. Whatever happened to the days of people making their own entertainment? Young people now have no initiative and I for one fail to see how throwing this kind of money at the problem is going to get them off their idle backsides.' (Hubert Trumper, 58)

- I only hope the money doesn't all go on kids. Don't they have enough entertainment these days? What we need are some clubs for the pensioners.' (George Adams, 67)

- 'Ridiculous idea! They'll soon change their tune when they see the problems it will cause – noisy groups of youngsters milling around these so-called community centres, getting up to no good and generally upsetting the local residents.' (Eileen Stern, 43)

- 'As a local community worker I welcome any idea which will focus people's activities on the community. But I hope that it will be organized so that people have a say in what happens in their own area. Too many good ideas fail through being bogged down in red tape at the civic centre.' (Peter Davis, 43)

Table 1: **Population statistics within the council's area**

Total population.	138,967
Percentages of people by age group	
under 16	18%
16–20	9
21–30	17
31–40	12
41–50	9
51–60	9
61–70	17
over 70	9

Explanation of above figures: The town has increased in size in the last 10 years through an influx of young families attracted by a government industrial expansion scheme. Thus there is an unusual mix of elderly people, many over retirement age, and relatively young families. Unemployment is above the national average but is concentrated mostly in the 40–60 age group. See also the map of the area.

Map of the area

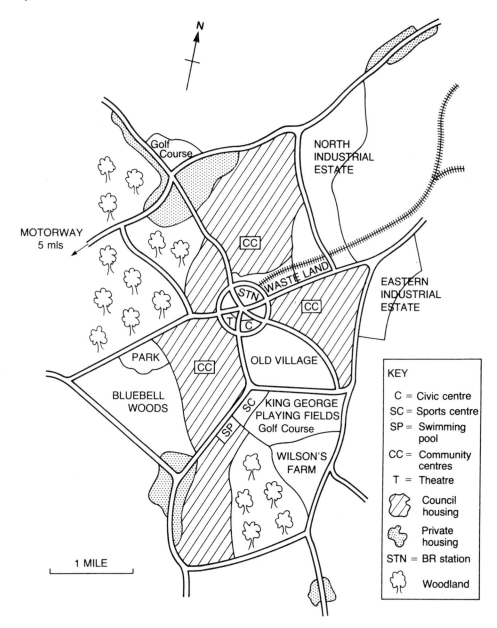

Table 2: **Current expenditure on leisure facilities with receipts from same**

	Expenditure	Income
Urban parks and open spaces	£187,789	£28,564
Indoor sports halls and leisure centres	65,678	32,187
Outdoor sports facilities	23,495	6,751
Theatre	3,234	1,089
Community centres	19,375	6,864
Golf course	10,486	7,865
Allotments	1,786	1,008
Miscellaneous (summer play groups, etc.) and administration costs	39,276	—
Totals	£351,119	£84,328

Table 3: **Cost of providing selected leisure facilities**

Building a new community centre to include seating for 100 in main hall, office and smaller room space, a snack bar and licensed bar: £250,000–£325,000 dependent on standard of decor etc.

A full leisure and sports centre to include space for skating rink, combined football/hockey/basketball etc. area, squash courts, sauna and bar plus one all-weather, all-purpose outdoor sports pitch: £3,750,000

15-seater Mini-bus equipped for elderly/disabled: £12,750 plus annual running cost of £1,350

Cost to council of providing extra, free bus services for OAPs and unemployed to run between estates and town centre 10am to 4 pm: (annually) £43,500

Your job now is to be the working party and decide on how to get the best use out of the money available. Bear in mind the comment that it is a good idea to spend more money 'if it is done right'.

1 In small groups, draw up a policy statement. Discuss the information given above then make notes on areas where you think more money could be spent. Include as well any new schemes you think are needed. The policy statement should be simply your outline plans for the *type* of provision you think is necessary. It should include the following:

● Which group or groups of people you are providing for.
● Any schemes you think could earn money, or any charges you would raise to help finance the scheme.
● Any 'change of use' of existing buildings which would make more economical use of them, such as opening schools at night for leisure classes.

2 Now present your ideas to the rest of the class. Then make notes on any ideas you did not think of and which you would add into your own schemes.

3 Now draw up a final report to be presented to the council detailing:
- Expansion of existing schemes.
- Introduction of new ideas.
- The groups who will benefit.
- Any spending which will be a 'once and for all' expense such as building a new community centre.

4 If your scheme is accepted you will have to let people know about it. Design a poster or full-page advert for the local paper that will inform people of the changes and encourage them to use the facilities provided.

9

Spaceship earth

By the end of this chapter the student should be able to:
1 Recognise the importance of the natural environment.
2 Assess the extent to which human interference damages the natural world.
3 Recognise the impact of the advanced economies on the rest of the world.
4 Suggest ways in which this impact may be reduced.
5 Recognise the need for greater awareness of environmental issues.

Below is a list of items we take for granted as part of modern living.

- Cars
- Television and video
- Hi-fi stereo systems
- Telephones
- Microwave ovens

- Washing machines
- Refrigerators/freezers
- Electric light
- Computers
- Central heating

Even if we do not have all of these things we are at least familiar with most of them, yet fifty years ago very few people owned any of them and some were unheard of.

At least, this is true for a society like Britain, but not for many of the world's poorer countries, because high technology items like these are very unevenly distributed around the world. And one thing you may notice about them is that to work they all require some form of energy – electricity, petrol or gas.

In general terms it is estimated that one-quarter of the world's population uses three-quarters of its natural resources, either to make the sort of items listed above or in the production of energy.

Can you guess which countries would be included in this one-quarter?

The scale of industrial production in the United States is so great that companies like Ford and Coca-Cola have a higher turnover of money than some countries.

So two things that give a clue to how advanced a society is would be its consumption of *energy* and *natural resources*.

▶ ▶ ▶ ▶ **SOMETHING TO DO**

Try to imagine what life would be like without electricity. (You could discuss this in small groups to bring more ideas together.)

As a starting point think about the things in the home you would have to go without.

Then think about the goods that form part of your normal life such as clothes and food which are made in factories using electric power.

As you go on you may find that there are:

- Things you would lose altogether, such as television.
- Things you would have to do differently such as eating fresh, not frozen, food.
- Things which would not change at all, such as . . . well, what?

Eventually you may give up trying to imagine what life would be like simply because it would be so different. But perhaps this has given you an idea of what it would have been like to have lived a hundred years ago; or what it is like living in one of the poorer countries of the world today.

But what are the chances of the electricity supply just 'running out'?

In Britain the Central Electricity Generating Board is responsible for producing power which it distributes around the country via the National Grid system. The power stations used for this mostly have to use a fuel that heats water and turns it to steam which in turn drives large generators or turbines. The fuels used to do this are mostly:

- Coal
- Oil and gas
- Nuclear

At the moment the most commonly used fuel is coal but nuclear power is planned to be a much bigger provider of energy in the future as can be seen in the figure on page 120.

You will notice that the area for oil-fired stations dwindles away to nothing by the year 2020. This is because the world's supply of oil is expected to run out by then, at least in any useful quantities. And this is part of a much larger problem. While we want to carry on expanding our industries and our use of goods to improve our life-styles, we are using up the world's supply of raw materials at an alarming rate.

This is why this chapter is called 'Spaceship earth'. It is an expression coined some years ago to illustrate the fact that we are like travellers on a spaceship and that all the things we have are what we carry with us. Once the raw materials run out, like iron for example, there is no way of getting any more. It will be gone forever.

Oil is a *fossil fuel*. It is made up of the decomposed remains of minute sea creatures which died millions of years ago, sank to the bottom of the sea and became trapped in sedimentary rock. Natural gas is also usually found with oil fields.

Where we get our electricity from and how this will change

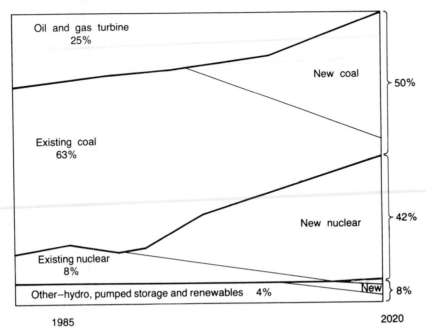

Source: Adapted from John Baker, *Nuclear Electricity*, CEGB, 1985.

Oil has only been useful since about 1900 when road, and later air, transport pushed up the demand. (Before this, American farmers who found oil on their land would sell the land at rock bottom prices because they thought it a nuisance.)

Apart from fuelling cars and power stations, oil is widely used in the production of plastics, fertilizers and synthetic fibres. So just about every aspect of our lives includes some dependence on oil – clothes, food, transport, domestic power.

The known reserves will last until about 2025, which means that something that took millions of years to make will have gone in just over a century.

This highlights a problem that was given the name 'The Tragedy of the Commons'. This is a situation that occurs when there is a limited supply of something – food, for example. If everybody takes whatever they can, then for a short while they will all have what they want, but as the supply dries up everyone suffers.

BUT . . .

If one person, who can see what is about to happen, cuts down on his consumption to save existing reserves then everyone else will get more than him and supplies will run out anyway.

If everyone cuts back, then one person taking more than his fair share will make no difference.

In other words, it seems as though the selfish ones will win or at least be no worse off than anyone else.

This is what the developed part of the world seems to be doing with the supply of natural resources.

▶ ▶ ▶ ▶ SOMETHING TO DO

Try the following game called 'The Prisoner's Dilemma'. It is quite simple.

All you have to do is choose C or D while your playing partner does the same. Write your choice down but do not let your partner know what you have chosen. One of you is Red while the other is Blue.

A referee then looks at what you both wrote down, tells you and then you read off what you score by looking across the rows and columns:

- If you choose C and your partner chooses C you both score 3.
- If you choose D and your partner chooses D you both score 2.
- If you choose D and your partner chooses C you score 4, your partner scores 1 – and vice versa.

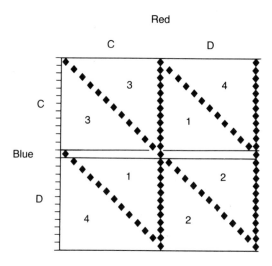

Play the game:

1 Against each other. That is, try to get the best score you can for yourself.
2 In teams of two. In other words, add up both scores after, say, ten rounds and take your combined scores, then let two others have a go. The winning team has the highest combined players' scores.

How long did it take you to realize that, if you play perhaps ten or twenty times and add up the scores, the best individual scores would be if you both chose C, even though you can lose if your partner keeps playing D?

In this game at least, the way to win is to co-operate.

► ► ► ► **TALKING POINT**

- Is it in everyone's interest to co-operate in other things as well? Or do we carry on trying to 'win' all the time in the (perhaps mistaken) belief that we must compete to succeed?

If you play a game you expect that everyone involved will stick to the rules. If you can make the rules up as you go along that will obviously give you an advantage. This kind of unequal competition is what Richard North highlights in an article in the *Sunday Times* magazine of 10 August 1986. Here is an extract:

> . . . the rich world buys a tremendous range of products from poor countries and we – the rich – pay too little for them. More damaging still, we organise tariff barriers and subsidies for our own farmers in such a way that farmers in poor countries stand little chance of developing a healthy export trade. The rich world spends about US$65 billion a year subsidising its farmers. Ironically, that is about the same as the poor countries lost during 1984–5 as the price of their commodities slipped on world markets.
>
> The World Bank, horrified at the inequities in world trade, argues forcefully for freer markets. A word of caution, however: as trade develops between poor countries and rich, it will almost certainly benefit the rich elites in the poor countries long before it touches the real poor.
>
> In most poor, hot countries, the men and women who are closest to the land (especially the women who do much of the hardest work on peasant farms) are furthest from any decent reward. The rich countries could make their most effective contribution by agreeing financial assistance to Third World governments only in return for policies designed to ensure that the hands that grow the food get the reward. That means fewer Mercedes Benz cars for government officials and many more water taps for the villagers.
>
> We are a very long way from achieving a world economy which is even halfway geared to the needs of the poor. For many years yet the price at the supermarket check-out will not begin to represent the *real* cost of our goods to the planet.

The article also includes some examples of what it takes to produce certain goods. The following examples are adapted from the article.

> Since the 1950s we have doubled the number of passenger kilometres travelled in Britain. (A passenger kilometre is one person travelling 1 kilometre – thus three people travelling together in a car for 100 kilometres is 300 passenger kilometres.)
>
> But the train (ideal for most long journeys), the bus (ideal for shorter journeys), and the bicycle (ideal for the shortest journeys) have all seen dramatic declines, both in their share of the total and in the overall number of passenger kilometres they deliver. The car reigns supreme.
>
> More than half the cars taking people to work travel less than 5 miles;
>
> More than 80% carry only one person;
>
> Cars and lorries dump more than 9 million tonnes of pollution into the environment every year;

But cars do not provide mobility for all – only about a third of the poorer households are car owning.

Our changing travel habits: total passenger kilometres and percentages of types of transport used

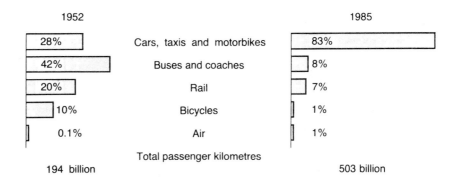

1952		1985
28%	Cars, taxis and motorbikes	83%
42%	Buses and coaches	8%
20%	Rail	7%
10%	Bicycles	1%
0.1%	Air	1%

Total passenger kilometres

194 billion   503 billion

• Do you have any pets?

The average contented cat is a considerable eater, demanding about a third more calories, weight for weight, than its owner. A 4 kg cat eats about 350 kilocalories of animal protein a day – twice as much as an average African and better than a third more than the average citizen of the Third World. The money spent on its upkeep – around £170 per year – is greater than the *per capita* gross national product of the billion-plus people who live in the world's fifteen poorest countries.

Basically this means that we spend more on looking after our pets than some people – about a quarter of the world's population – actually earn.

• Are you wearing jeans?

About 0.75 kg of cotton goes into making a pair of jeans. It is by far the world's most common non-food crop, grown on around 30 million hectares. It is back-breaking work and dangerous – the workers are in constant contact with very powerful insecticides.

But in addition to the cotton – one bale of 218 kg will make 330 pairs – their production also uses up:

• 398,000 litres of water
• 30 litres of petrol
• 61 litres of diesel fuel
• 7.6 litres of liquid propane gas
• 60 kilowatt-hours of electricity
• 64 cubic metres of natural gas
• 14 kg of nitrogen
• 6.8 kg of phosphate
• 10.9 kg of potash

And if one Levi's advert is to be believed, half a mountain has to be blown up to make the copper rivets.

► ► ► ► **TALKING POINT**

Do you feel any sense of guilt or even anger at these facts and figures?

► ► ► ► **SOMETHING TO DO**

In groups imagine that you are one of the following people:

1 A British importer who buys goods and raw materials from the Third World countries and sells them on the markets in Britain.
2 A British politician who is part of a committee looking into giving more aid to Third World countries.
3 A pensioner who is worried about the price of goods in the shops.
4 A journalist who has just come back from Central Africa where you have seen widespread starvation.

The information above has just been given to you. How do you think you would react? What are your feelings about it?

Remember: each of these people has different aims in life from wanting lower prices to seeking publicity and profit from what they do.
So . . .

● Take five minutes or so discussing how you think this person would react.
● Tell the rest of the class.
● Then, still imagining that you are this person, you are told that the government is going to take steps, along with other countries, to try to change the situation and produce more equality in international trade, which could mean higher prices, lower profits, fewer goods.
● What is your reaction?
● Again, state how you feel, then discuss your reasons for supporting or opposing such a proposal.

What a load of rubbish

You have probably seen the 'Save It' campaign stickers and symbols and, more recently, the 'Monergy' slogan.

It is interesting that the very people whose business it is to sell energy (the CEGB) are asking us to cut down by using it more efficiently, particularly through insulating our homes. Yet while car manufacturers try to make engines more efficient they still do not build cars meant to last for 20 years or more, even though they could for little extra cost. Why?

▶ ▶ ▶ ▶ **FACT**

In the United States 9 million cars are scrapped every year. Is the iron or steel from which they are made so plentiful that we can afford to waste it? It is not just the raw materials that are wasted – it is also all the energy that went into making the goods in the first place.

▶ ▶ ▶ ▶ **SOMETHING TO DO**

List five (or more) household items, then write down:

1 What they are made of.
2 How much they cost.
3 How long you would expect them to last.
4 What resources are used up to keep them going (e.g. electricity).
5 What can still be recovered at the end of their useful life.

Here is an example

Item	1	2	3	4	5
Car	Steel, rubber, glass, plastics, vinyl, (from oil)	£5,000+	10 years	Oil plus spare parts as in 1	Scrap metals

Waste is a major problem and it can take many forms. Every household in Britain produces 1.5 tonnes of waste each year, about a third of which is packaging –boxes, cans, bottles.

Factories produce waste. It may be just what is lost in the process of turning raw materials into finished items, or the by-products of a process.

Power production, which uses coal, oil and nuclear fuel, produces a variety of waste, most of which is dangerous to life. And then, if we don't use that energy efficiently by insulating our homes, even the raw materials are wasted.

Packaging and the environment

Much of what we buy is wasted simply because it is used only for the packaging of the goods. Do an average weeks shopping in a supermarket and you will come away with a vast array of paper, plastic, metal and glass packaging which is likely to be used once (on the journey home and for storage afterwards) then thrown away.

Some of these products may be *bio-degradable* – that is, they will break down naturally into their component parts through the action of bacteria in the soil. Others may be *re-usable*.

Paper is degradable*, but has limited re-use in its original form; it would need to be re-cycled first. Paper is about the easiest of products to re-cycle, in fact, yet we manage to reclaim less than 10% of it. This is despite the fact that it takes about 17 fully grown trees to make one tonne of paper.

Plastics such as polythene, polystyrene and PVC are not degradable. Some plastics can be re-used but this is made difficult because it is very costly or difficult to reclaim from household waste, mixed in as it is with all the other rubbish. It is made from oil products, and the oil is is rappidly running out, so every carrier bag you throw away after using once is adding to the depletion of the world's oil.

Metals vary, but when steel degrades it turns into rust and is useless. Aluminium does not degrade. Metals cannot normally be re-used in their original form but may be re-cycled – many of Britain's weapons in the Second World War were made from old saucepans and iron railings. If we had the will in peacetime we could save a great deal of our natural resources.

Glass in the form of bottles and jars can be re-cycled, although this uses a great deal of energy. They can of course be re-used, but glass which is dumped is not degradable.

And what about the energy and resources taken to make these goods in the first place? Take paper, for example. Every tonne of paper we produce uses up

- 17 fully grown trees
- 125 kg of sulphur
- 160 kg of limestone
- 280,000 litres of water
- 4000 kg of steam
- 255 kilowatt-hours of electricity

less than one-tenth of which is reclaimed, even though paper is one of the easiest products to re-cycle.

The case of the vanishing lead

Question: What would you do if you wanted to hide 10,000 tonnes of lead?
Answer: Put it in petrol and let the motor car pump it into the air. This is what cars do every year in Britain. The lead is added to the petrol as an 'anti-knock' additive for smoother running and is simply passed out of the exhaust into the atmosphere. You may have noticed that in America there is a move towards lead-free petrol to cut down on the pollution of their major cities.

---

* Degradability means whether the substance will be broken down by natural means such as bacteria in the soil. Thus paper will eventually return to its natural constituents while glass and aluminium will remain as they are.

Pollution takes many forms. Here are a few examples:

- Rivers suffer many problems of pollution by industrial and even agricultural wastes.

  The Rhine in Germany takes vast quantities of waste from the many factories which line its bank. There are so many chemicals in it that it is possible to develop a photographic plate in the waters of its estuary.

  In the United States there is a river that is so polluted it has to be watched constantly in case it *catches fire*.

  Fertilisers used in large-scale agriculture often wash off the fields and find their way into rivers and drinking water; this can harm unborn babies and cause cancer.

- Seas and oceans don't do much better – after all, what gets into a river will eventually find its way into the sea.

  Apart from this there is the problem of ships at sea that throw their rubbish overboard, or huge oil tankers that flush their tanks at sea or are involved in serious accidents. On an ocean voyage of 54 days, Thor Heyerdal reported seeing oil pollution on 47 of them.

  Fish caught in some seas are unfit to eat because they contain dangerous levels of mercury. Fish caught in the Irish Sea near Sellafield may even be radioactive.

- Air pollution takes many forms. As well as lead, cars put carbon monoxide and carbon dioxide into the air. They use up resources as well. If you take into account all the energy that goes into making petrol from crude oil; then realize that only about one-third of the energy from a gallon of petrol is used in moving the car (the rest is lost in heat and exhaust), then a car actually uses about 6 per cent of the available energy in the oil.

  And what it gives to the atmosphere in pollution it takes away in other areas. When a car does a journey of 600 miles it uses up more oxygen than a human being does in a lifetime.

  Just living in New York city and therefore breathing its air is the equivalent of smoking twenty cigarettes a day.

  In Britain there are regulations governing the height of chimney stacks so that pollution is taken high into the atmosphere and dispersed. This does save on local pollution but has the unfortunate effect of moving it somewhere else. Countries like Norway and Sweden suffer the pollution, in the form of acid rain, produced in places like Sheffield, Newcastle and Middlesbrough.

  Since 1945 there has been an increase in radioactivity levels around the world from nuclear weapons testing. If you drill into the ice in Greenland you can tell which layer was formed in 1945 – it shows an increase in radiation which was the result of Hiroshima and Nagasaki.

- Power generation. We have already seen how hungry some nations can be in their consumption of energy, and while gas and electricity may appear to be 'clean' in the home or factory, the power stations and organizations that produce it for us also produce vast amounts of pollutants – smoke, sulphur dioxide which

produces acid rain, unsightly and dangerous slag heaps, highly dangerous radioactive waste . . .
AND SO ON . . .

There are so many facts and figures that could be used to show the damage we are doing to our planet it would take a separate book to do justice to the subject. There are many sources of information, however, some of which are listed below if you would like to know more.

- *Earth in Danger* by Ian Breach and Michael Crawford (Book Club Associates, Smith/Doubleday House, 87 Newman St, London W1P 4EN).
- *The Real Cost* by Richard North (Chatto & Windus, London).
- Various Study Notes from The Conservation Trust, 246 London Road, Earley, Reading, RG6 1AG.

But there are also some things you might like to find out for yourself.

▶ ▶ ▶ ▶ **SOMETHING TO DO**

Find out how wasteful (or not) people can be with energy.
Try the following survey, either on the staff of your school/college or on the general public.

Occupation (then place in category in Chapter 1, p. 10) . . . .
Age   16–25 ☐ 26–35 ☐ 36–45 ☐ 46–55 ☐ 56–65 ☐ over 65 ☐ (Tick one)
Are you   Owner-occupier ☐ Council tenant ☐ Private tenant ☐ Other ☐

Part 1 TRANSPORT

1 Do you own a car?   Yes ☐ No ☐
   If yes answer questions 2 to 7; if no answer questions 7 to 11.

2 How do you get to work?
   Car ☐ Train ☐ Bicycle ☐ Bus ☐ Walk ☐ Other* ☐

3 How many miles per year would you estimate you travel in your car?
   Under 5,000 ☐ 5,000–8,000 ☐ 8,000–12,000 ☐ Over 12,000 ☐

4 What is the car's engine size?
   Under 1,200 cc ☐ 1,200–1,800 cc ☐ 1,800 –2,500 cc ☐ over 2,500 cc ☐

5 What would you estimate to be your average petrol consumption?
   Over 40 mpg ☐ 35–40 mpg ☐ 30–35 mpg ☐ 25–30 mpg ☐ 20–25 mpg ☐ Under 20 mpg ☐

6 How old is your car?
   Under 1 yr ☐ 1–3 yrs ☐ 4–6 yrs ☐ Over 6 yrs ☐

7 How often do you use public transport?
   Often (more than twice a week) ☐ About once a week ☐
   Two or three times a month ☐ About once a month ☐ Hardly ever ☐

8 How do you get to work?
Car ☐ Train ☐ Bicycle ☐ Bus ☐ Walk ☐ Other* ☐

9 Do you have use of a car?   Yes ☐ No ☐

10 If yes, when?
Evenings ☐ Weekends ☐ Day ☐

11 Which form of transport do you use most often?
Bus ☐ Train ☐ Bicycle ☐ Walk ☐ Taxi ☐ Other ☐

* Include unemployed here.

Part 2 IN THE HOME

1 Which of the following do you use at home for heating?
Gas ☐ Electricity ☐ Oil ☐ Solid fuel ☐ Other ☐

2 Which do you use for cooking?
Gas ☐ Electricity ☐ Solid fuel ☐ Other ☐

3 Which of the following domestic appliances do you have?
Automatic washing machine ☐ Refrigerator ☐
Freezer ☐ Microwave oven ☐ Dishwasher ☐
Toaster ☐ Colour television ☐ Video ☐

4 Do you have central heating?   Yes ☐ No ☐

5 Which of the following insulation do you have?
Loft insulation ☐ Water heater jacket ☐
Double glazing ☐ Cavity wall insulation ☐
Door and window draught excluders ☐ Porch ☐

6 What do you think is a reasonable temperature for your home?
15 °C ☐ 16 °C ☐ 17 °C ☐ 18 °C ☐ 19 °C ☐ 20 °C ☐ 21 °C ☐ 22 °C ☐ 23 °C ☐
59 °F ☐ 61 °F ☐ 63 °F ☐ 64 °F ☐ 66 °F ☐ 68 °F ☐ 70 °F ☐ 72 °F ☐ 73 °F ☐

Part 3 GENERAL

1 Which of the following do you believe are major problems or issues in modern society?
Air pollution ☐ Acid rain ☐ Litter ☐ Noise ☐ Energy conservation ☐
Nuclear waste ☐ Road Transport ☐

2 Do you think the government should do more to educate the public about pollution?
Yes ☐ No ☐ Don't know ☐

3 Do you think that pollution is sufficiently serious to endanger life on earth –
(a) now?   Yes ☐ No ☐ Don't know ☐
(b) in the near future?   Yes ☐ No ☐ Don't know ☐

You can now make your analysis of the results as simple or as complicated as you wish. Add questions if you would like to find out more about how people feel.

One suggestion would be to look at the results by occupation and age. Are people in the higher paid jobs more knowledgeable about the issues? Do younger people know more? Do people really care? You might like to include questions that ask how much people would be willing to give up now to make sure of our survival in the future.

One of the major debates at present on environmental issues is that of *nuclear power*.

The two main arguments are:

1 It is clean, safe and inexpensive.
   We need it.
2 It is dangerous, possibly disastrous.
   We wouldn't need it if we explored alternatives and saved energy anyway.

But it is much more complicated than this. Governments like it because it saves us from being dependent on coal and oil, both of which have given problems of supply and price in the past. Some people dislike the fact that nuclear power can also be used to make nuclear weapons.

The issues are too complicated to be dealt with here because of the lack of space, but you might wish to contact the CEGB Public Relations office at

CEGB Department of Information and Public Affairs
Sudbury House
15 Newgate Street
London EC1A 7AU

They produce some excellent booklets on nuclear and other energy, including the so-called 'alternative energy' sources.

But to balance this you might also like to get information from

- The Conservation Trust
- Friends of the Earth
- Greenpeace

—10—

Whose side are you on?

By the end of this chapter the student should be able to:
1 Evaluate the effect of stereotyping on conflict situations.
2 Suggest reasons for conflict between people and groups.
3 Assess ways in which conflict may be reduced.
4 Examine situations in which he/she comes into conflict with others.
5 Assess his/her contribution to the existence of such conflict.

Our lives are full of conflicts. Most of them are minor ones, such as disagreements in the home or at work and they soon pass. Others are more serious and long-lasting, such as racial conflicts within communities, and at the most serious level countries may go to war with each other. Conflicts are very often presented to us as being one side against another, but the larger they are the more complicated they become. The political conflicts in Northern Ireland and Palestine, for example, have grown out of very complex circumstances and so do not have any neat, easy solution even though there are always people around who like to offer simple answers.

The whole point of this book has been to look at as many different points of view as possible. So to finish off, here is a general look at just a few more.

Very classy

Is Britain divided into social classes which are always in conflict with each other? People even disagree over this question. Few people, though, would deny the existence of huge differences in wealth and income between groups of people – one-parent families on social security and millionaire businessmen, for example.

But does this mean that there are a few obvious groups which are in some kind of conflict with each other?

Are some people doing well *at the expense of others* and, more important, doing so *deliberately*?

▶ ▶ ▶ ▶ SOMETHING TO DO

Divide into groups and discuss how you would define a 'social class', then make a note of what you base this definition on.

For example, if you use the expressions 'working', 'middle' and 'upper class', how do you decide who to fit into them?

Is it money, wealth, attitudes? Or none of these?

Then explain your ideas to the rest of the class.

▶ ▶ ▶ ▶ THE POINT IS . . .

Different societies have different ways of grouping people. In Britain and other industrial societies the basis of our differences is mostly the job we do, the money we earn and the life-style this brings us. Because this does not define who *should* be in a particular place in society, some people believe that there is no such thing as 'class conflict'. You probably also found that some of you objected to the whole idea of classifying people in this way.

But in other countries there are rules and laws that mean that people *are* made to live a certain way.

In India, the caste system, where it exists, is based on an accident of birth. You are born into a particular caste and there you stay for life. This means that your chances in life are strictly limited. The basis of this is the organization of people through religion – the top caste are priests.

In South Africa there is a different system which has a similar aim and effect. You are defined by race – white, coloured and black – and the law strictly limits what you are allowed to do, keeping people separate and denying many of them the power over their own lives.

▶ ▶ ▶ ▶ **TALKING POINT**

Are there any similarities between these systems and Britain?

In South Africa the system is designed to keep power in the hands of a minority. This is done by rules backed up with force.

If the basis of divisions in Britain is success in getting a good job and earning money, it could be argued that if some people are not allowed the chance to get on and do well, then a class system designed to favour one group really does exist.

Does this happen?

Or do we all have equal chances to do well?

Whatever your views on this, the political life of Britain is based on this argument.

Basically, politics is about *who* decides *what* and for *whose benefit*.

In a dictatorship these questions are easily answered – one person, or a small group of people, decide everything for the benefit of themselves and a small section of society. Those who object are normally stopped by force.

Britain is a democracy. Everyone of 18 and over is allowed to choose the people who will run the country for us. We have elections at least every 5 years and then the party we choose is given the job of putting its ideas into practice. All of them tell us that what they do is for the benefit of us all.

Is this true?

▶ ▶ ▶ ▶ **SOMETHING TO DO**

1 Divide into groups and look at the parties using the definition of politics above.

It doesn't matter if you don't think you know much about politics – the important thing is what you *think* the parties stand for.

Make a note of:

● Who – what type of people belong to this party and vote for them?
● What – what types of policies do you associate with them?
● Who benefits – everyone? Or a certain section of society?

The main parties in this country are Conservative, Labour and the Social and Liberal Democrats, but you can do this for other parties as well. These might include the National Front, the Socialist Workers' Party, the Communist Party, the Green Party and also any parties which exist where you live, such as Welsh and Scottish Nationalists or the Ulster parties.

You may find this more difficult because of the little publicity the smaller parties receive.

2 When you have done this, discuss your ideas as a class – *not* in terms of whether the policies are good or bad, but just on whether you agree that these parties do have these particular policies.

Eventually you should come up with a set of ideas that fit in with what the various parties stand for.

3 Now divide into groups again, but this time each group is one of the political

parties. (It doesn't matter if you are in a 'party' you disagree with – in fact it may be better.)

4 Look at the following proposals and produce a policy statement on each one. That is, state what you think *your* party would do if it was in power and had to decide on what action to take.

- Bring back hanging for terrorists who commit murder.
- Spend more money on social security – increased unemployment benefit, pensions and supplementary benefits.
- Introduce very heavy fines for firms who pollute the countryside with industrial waste.
- Introduce much tougher penalties for crimes of violence.
- Scrap Britain's nuclear weapons.

You might also like to add some current issues and look at them in this way.

Does a consistent pattern emerge within a party over its approach to problems?

One of the age-old issues of politics is the problem of a conflict between the state and the individual.

If we want to allow people freedom in a society, how do we draw the line between what is and isn't acceptable?

Freedom is a 'good' word. Politicians love to use it. But if one person's freedom is another person's slavery, can we accept that as a way of life?

In practice we tend to accept that people should be allowed to run their own lives as long as the way they do it does no harm to anyone else. If it does then we pass laws which put a stop to it.

In reality, of course, society does not consist of individuals who somehow make up a nation or state. It is a collection of groups of people who share common interests and experiences of life.

The smallest of these groups is the basic family unit of parents and children. Then there are larger groups such as firms where, as we've seen, there may be a conflict of interest between workers and management. There are clubs for leisure activities; local community organizations; national groups such as ethnic minorities and pensioners; trade unions; employers' and business organizations; the unemployed; young people, and so on. Each of them has a set of interests and expectations of how they should be treated.

And they are each bidding in some way for a favourable share of what society as a whole has to offer.

And is it really only the political parties who claim to have the answers to keep everyone happy?

Sugar and spice and all things sexist

Of course, the politicians can pass laws for ever more, but if these laws mean changes to people's lives or routines, they may meet resistance. The fact that a thing was always done a particular way doesn't necessarily mean that it was right for everyone. But if people feel that their life is being changed in some way, or, worse, if they feel they are now being told they were *wrong* to do what they did in the past, it will take time for them to get used to the new ideas.

So what happens when a law goes against people's attitudes and prejudices? Let's look at the case of women.

In 1975 it became illegal for anyone to discriminate against a person merely on the grounds of sex. While this applies to both men and women, it was seen as a first step in improving the status of women in society since they were the ones who had suffered the discrimination in the past – lower wages, fewer opportunities and prejudice which said that a woman's place was in the home. Suddenly the law recognized that women were equal and of course many men now found their traditional ideas being challenged.

How do you feel about this?

▶ ▶ ▶ ▶ SOMETHING TO DO

1 Make three lists of five jobs.

The first should be the types of jobs normally done by women.

The second should be a list of jobs you think women could do but are normally done by men.

The third should be a list of jobs you think women would do better than men.

Be prepared to give reasons for what you include on your lists.

2 List the jobs in and around the home you think should be done by men and by women.

Now list the functions in a family that *can only be done* by men or women.

Make a set of class lists to include the information you all thought of.

How traditional were you?

Do you feel, for example, that women do particular jobs because they are better at them than men?

Just because a situation exists, does that mean that it *ought to be* that way?

Would you be surprised to learn that when typewriters were first invented it was men who were given the job of using them? It was thought at the time that they were too technical for women to understand.

If you really do feel that a woman's place is in the home, how do you feel about being told that (a) it is illegal to try to act on this attitude by making it impossible (or very difficult) for women to succeed in a career, and (b) that you are wrong to think this way in the first place?

If on the other hand you believe that women are equal and should be given every opportunity to decide for themselves what they want to do, how do you feel about imposing your attitude on people who do not think the way you do?

▶ ▶ ▶ ▶ THE POINT IS . . .

Is there a point at which society has to decide to upset some of its members because there is a *moral* issue at stake?

Many laws are passed that are aimed at changing people's behaviour – you must not steal, kill, set fire to homes, and so on. These kinds of laws mean that people do not suffer for the actions of others, and most of us accept that it is *wrong* to offend in this way.

But will these kinds of rules change people's *attitudes*?

Will a future society accept it as perfectly normal that women are absolutely equal?

This idea of changing attitudes as well as actions is what gives rise to the kinds of stories we read in the newspapers, where people try to back up the laws with campaigns to make us think differently about the issue.

These campaigns are often treated as comical or ridiculous by the press. (What does this say about *their* attitudes?)

For example, there have been campaigns aimed at

(a) Changing the language we use so as to recognize the fact that women are equal. What, for example, is 'wrong' with the following words and expressions?

- Man-made fibre
- Male nurse
- Woman doctor
- Mankind
- Chairman
- Chairperson
- 'Caution – men working at rear' (sign on the front of various council vehicles)
- Manpower Services Commission

Have you seen any more examples like this?

(b) Positive discrimination. This involves giving jobs to women *before* men as long as they are qualified to do them. A local council in 1986, for example, provided jobs in construction for women only.

What do you think is the idea behind this type of action?

(c) Changing educational methods and materials, traditional fairy tales, for example, to show women as independent and equal. Instead of spending their lives waiting for 'Mr Right' to come along in the shape of a handsome prince, women are given a role in which they make things happen for themselves.

Perhaps you could re-write some nursery rhymes or fairy tales to reflect this change in attitudes.

As we've seen earlier, school has a very important role in shaping people for the future and preparing them for adult life. Are the schools now giving a more equal education to boys and girls alike?

Do you feel there are any subjects that are mostly for boys or girls, such as science, woodwork, home economics, secretarial studies?

▶ ▶ ▶ ▶ SOMETHING TO DO

A record by Boris Gardner that was successful at the end of 1986 contained the lines:

> You're everything a woman ought to be,
> Sweet and kind and pure of mind and beautiful to see.

Was he right?

Make a list of characteristics you think are typically female or typically male – personality, emotions, behaviour.

When you have done this, discuss them in class.

Can you honestly say that what you wrote down applies to *every* male or female in *every* situation?

If it doesn't, can you still accept that it is something 'natural', or is it possible to change people's attitudes?

Some of my best friends are racist

If it's possible to discriminate against about half the population of a country then it ought to be easier to do so with minority groups.

Racism is discrimination against a particular racial or ethnic group and is often made easier by the fact that these groups' languages and accents, skin colours or dress make them obvious.

Like all forms of discrimination it is based on certain *assumptions* which are made about groups as a whole.

For example, can you identify the following nationalities from the descriptions?

1 Efficient, arrogant, war-loving and they produce good scientists.
2 Mean with money, good in business and they stick together.
3 Brash, rich, competitive.
4 Excitable, romantic, cowardly in war but produce lots of gangsters.
5 Loutish lager drinkers who hate the British.
6 Thick drunks who build roads.
7 Cool, lazy, violent, marijuana smokers.
8 Timid, work all hours, stick together in tightly knit families.
9 Poor, dull and boring, want to conquer the world.

And finally – Reserved, violent, polite, arrogant, strongly nationalistic, drink too much, non-competitive, lazy, good at sports, bad losers, poor lovers.

▶ ▶ ▶ ▶ THE POINT IS . . .

There are no right answers here because there are no races of people who are like this – it's just that some people may think they are.

If you recognized the last one as 'British' you may be right but you may also have noticed that they were contradictory – how can a nation be both polite and arrogant?

Simple really – just ask an American businessman, a Belgian bar owner, European holiday-makers and the Spanish police and between them they might come up with all of those characteristics. It depends on your point of view.

And it's much easier to have a point of view about people if you know them. Since it is impossible for us to know everyone from another country or culture, it is also impossible to be able to state definitely that *that individual* fits our idea of what they are all like.

Remember the stereotype from Chapter 1?

Of course, if you are determined to be a racist then you must have some evidence and information to back up your prejudice; so that when you want to make sweeping statements about wogs, coons, yids and dagoes you can *prove* that they are what you say they are.

So, here's . . .

▶ ▶ ▶ ▶   SOMETHING TO DO

Imagine that you have arrived in Britain from another country (or even another planet) and that you have physical and economic superiority. In other words, you are more powerful than the locals.

You are not a nasty group of people. You would like to convince yourself as well as others that dominating this race of people is for the good of everyone. (But if you were pushed, you would start breaking heads to keep control.)

So the thing to do is to design a systematic campaign against the British to convince the rest of the world that they are inferior.

1 In groups, discuss and note down all the weaknesses and bad characteristics you think you could use as examples of how inferior the British are.

   (If you find this difficult, just think in terms of what the rest of the world may actually think of us.)

   It doesn't matter if what you come up with is hard to prove or is even untrue. It is usually possible to produce evidence of some kind that will illustrate your point.

2 The next task is to set about proving a point and so you will need to change the laws of the country. This will give you a chance to upset the people enough for them to react in ways that will help to prove your point.

   For example, you have decided the British are violent. You therefore pass a law that makes football matches illegal. This will bring protests from the football fans and the demonstrations (with a little help from you) will get violent. Point proved. We were right to ban football – look what kind of people go to matches.

   By making it difficult for the British to do well at school you can prove that they are not intelligent, and so on . . .

3 What kind of changes did you make? Discuss your 'campaign' as a class.

   Did anything come up that you recognize as already happening in Britain to other groups of people?

   Was it difficult to find fault with yourself?

   Did you feel that it was 'untrue' or ridiculous?

There is an alternative exercise that is easier since your teacher will have to do all the work.

All you do is to put two sets of badges in a bag, one red, one blue (or any two different colours), then draw them out and pin them on yourself.

The teacher will then treat you according to your badge colour. He or she will make the choice of which colour will be the 'good' group and will then give better treatment to that group. The 'bad' group will get lower marks, be given less encouragement and generally regarded as a waste of time.

How do you think you would feel after a month or so of this?

You could also examine how discrimination could be applied to other groups of people such as the elderly.

▶ ▶ ▶ ▶ THE POINT IS . . .

Many of our prejudices lie beneath the surface. We often do not know that we are discriminating, or else we allow assumptions about various groups of people to go unchallenged. We may make no comment, for example, when a sports commentator tells us that Scots with ginger hair have a fiery temperament. When we see a red-haired Scottish footballer being sent off the pitch it is almost as though we expected it, ignoring the fact that many red-headed Scots may also be very calm and placid people.

▶ ▶ ▶ ▶ TALKING POINT

Could we approach racism in the same way as sex discrimination – changing language, educational methods and using positive discrimination?

In recent years the Labour Party has been involved in an argument about whether they should set up 'Black Sections'.

The people in favour of this argue it would be a group that could do positive work for black people, keeping a check on racist attitudes and pushing for more black MPs, councillors and so on.

The people who oppose the idea are not racists. They want to see equality for black people but they think that if you separate them out into a section of their own, other people will still see them as 'different'. They think the best chance of eliminating racism is through having black people working alongside whites and showing they are equal partners.

This of course can be applied to society as a whole.

Which do *you* think would be the best way to achieve equality for minority groups in society?

What is it good for?

We saw in the last chapter that the amount of money it would take to feed the world's starving for a year is about the same as that spent on weapons every fortnight.

War has been a favourite activity of the human race throughout recorded history. For one reason or another nations and other groups of people have found it necessary to settle their differences by using violence.

But why?

There is an old Chinese proverb that says that he who strikes the first blow admits that he has lost the argument. In other words, if we have to resort to violence it is because we have not been clever enough to resolve the problem.

Another point of view might well be that the people who decide on whether or not to go to war are not the ones who are likely to be in any immediate danger from it. That may have been true of both World Wars, and more recently the Falklands conflict, but it would be less true of a nuclear war.

It is also a fact that a very small number of people in Britain today have actually been involved in a war directly. (There are still many people alive today who lost family and loved ones in the Second World War, as well as Korea and the Falklands. But even the number of people who fought in those conflicts is quite small.)

▶ ▶ ▶ ▶ **SOMETHING TO DO**

The question of nuclear weapons and all that goes with them – deterrence theory, multilateral or unilateral disarmament, who would be the aggressor and in what circumstances would we use them – is a very complex issue.

In small groups note down the arguments in favour of unilateral disarmament (one country such as Britain getting rid of its nuclear weapons), the arguments against and also all the points raised you cannot decide on.

Try it to see how many questions you *cannot* answer, such as, 'If one country reduced or got rid of its weapons, what would the other countries do?'

Then discuss the points you raised as a class, listing them as 'for', 'against' and 'points of interest'.

War is a very emotional event.

You only have to look at the news coverage of the Falklands conflict, especially by the 'popular' press, and the output by Hollywood film makers to see the truth of this. Yet a veteran American soldier once described war as 'Long periods of boredom interrupted by brief moments of sheer terror.'

▶ ▶ ▶ ▶ **TALKING POINTS**

If you had the power to decide, under what circumstances would you as a leader of a country actually take the decision to declare war on another country?

Under what circumstances would you as an individual want to go to war?

Is war unavoidable? In other words, is it part of 'human nature' to be aggressive and want to impose power over others?

And going back to the Chinese proverb, do you agree with it?

Is war something that happens when people run out of arguments around the diplomatic table?

Or is it the logical next step when two nations disagree?

And finally, do you think it sensible to try to impose rules on how a war should be fought? The Geneva Convention, for example, has 'outlawed' certain types of weapon such as exploding bullets and chemical weapons. Does this make sense given that people are trying to find the best way they can to kill the enemy?

Why has this same body not outlawed nuclear weapons? After all, their effects are very nasty indeed.

As has been mentioned, war has been glamorized by Hollywood over the years with tales of heroism, glory and generally 'doing what a man's gotta do'. Here is a little reality.

The following are extracts from the diary of an RAF technician during the Second World War. He was sent out to North Africa in 1942 to follow the advance from there into Europe.

> *Nov. 27th*: Left Liverpool docks to make my weary way to N. Africa. Saw Scotland, Ireland, then days of the Atlantic . . .
>
> This day, Dec. 7th, marched with full kit to a disused brick field. Stayed one week, living on emergency rations. Bitterly cold at night.
>
> *Dec. 20th*: Our meals are a modern girl's delight. Tins! Boy, if only the war would finish and we could go home. Have been told that most insects out here are dangerous. Centipedes, spiders, mosquitoes, scorpions are all deadly. Bang! One centipede less. . . . Had tea. ½ tin sardines, biscuits and tea. Last smoke. Into bed at 7 o'clock. Late tonight.
>
> *Dec. 21st*: Digging trenches all morning. Have scrounged off for a moment. Boy! Am I cheesed! If the front line is a few miles off they don't worry about it . . . Have been swinging an axe, clearing a space for our beloved officers. Tea, lousy.
>
> *Dec. 22nd*: This being near Xmas, am allowed two cables home, one to mum and family, one to Mary. We don't write them. They are picked from a list (of standard phrases).
>
> *Dec. 23rd*: Breakfast. One sausage, biscuits. On 24 hour guard. Still raining! Manchester is a dry place by comparison. Some of the boys are laying telephone and electric cables. Lights for officers from latter. They think they are still at home. I'd like to send them to a better place which is hotter than any country. There have been some tenders arriving. Perhaps we'll get some technical work done. Tea is scarce. I think someone has been fiddling. They just don't worry about us here.
>
> *Dec. 25th*: Breakfast. One sausage, biscuits. Dinner. Same tripe! Buzzed off to town to get some scent. They can whistle for me!
>
> *Dec. 28th*: Tired and fed up. On fatigues after a wash and shave. Wrote a letter to Mary. Still waiting for parcel to be censored. Went to town. Still

cheesed off. Only alternative, Bed!

Jan. 1st 1943: Everybody getting soused at 1 a.m. On a DF wagon with a few blokes, charging acc's and generally making myself useful. Had a letter from Mary. Grub has improved after a hectic mess meeting. Exchanged my rifle for a Sten Gun. So to bed on the first day of 1943.

And so on . . .

This particular technician was quite lucky. There was very little sheer terror to interrupt the boredom. His brother was less fortunate. He was killed at Arnhem on his first day of active duty. The technician has not been to see the film *A Bridge Too Far*.

Conclusion

The aim of this book has been to try to illustrate some of the different points of view that apply to various situations.

It only remains to say that in most situations there are more than just two.

If we take the time and trouble to think about what we see, hear and read it might help us to avoid getting stuck in a rut of quick judgements and confrontations with others.

After all, we are supposed to be living in a society that works on the principle of, 'I may not agree with what you say but I will defend your right to say it.'